CW00740824

new city spaces

The research project "New Tendencies in Public Space
Architecture" was conducted from 1992-2000 at:

Centre for Public Space Research
Institute for Planning
School of Architecture
Royal Danish Academy of Fine Arts
Phillip de Langes Alle 10
DK-1435 Copenhagen K
Denmark

The project was made possible with the financial support
of the following institutions and foundations:

Direktør E. Danielsen og hustrus Fond
Margot og Thorvald Dreyers Fond
Fonden RealDania
The Danish Ministry of Culture

© The Danish Architectural Press
Jan Gehl and Lars Gemzøe,
Third edition
Copenhagen, 2003
English translation: Karen Steenhard
Layout: Stine Sandahl and Marie-Louise Teilmann
Editorial assistant: Zuhra Sasa
Repro: Arco Grafisk A/S, Denmark
Printing: Arco Grafisk A/S, Denmark
ISBN 87-7407-293-5

new city spaces

jan gehl & lars gemzøe

The Danish Architectural Press

Contents

39 streets and squares

Appendix

Foreword

Copenhagen is generally considered as a beacon of hope in terms of urban regeneration – one of the few true examples of a humanised European city where squares and streets have been thoughtfully and steadily enhanced over the last 30 years, offering the city a sequence of impressive and inspirational public spaces. Against this background Copenhagen provides an excellent platform from which to study and describe the new role and new form of public spaces in contemporary society.

This excellent new book is an illuminating account of the working methods used, showing the delicate analysis, identifying and mapping those elements of urban fabric that together constitute an energised whole. The book offers a fascinating and instructive insight into these working methods, and highlights particular examples of successful urban design that best serve the everyday needs of city communities. The vision ranges from the exact number of front doors within a given stretch of thoroughfare contributing to a lively street environment right through to the broad sweep of monumental public spaces, identifying surface treatments and lighting systems that will humanise and dramatise the urban landscape.

Jan Gehl and Lars Gemzøe believe passionately in the importance of citizenship and the liveliness and humanity it stimulates. This manifests itself in planned large-scale civic gestures but also in the small scale and the spontaneous which together create a rich diversity of city life. Cities remain the great demographic magnets of our time because they facilitate work and are the seedbeds of our cultural development. Cities are centres of communication, learning and complex commercial enterprises; they house huge concentrations of families; they focus and condense physical, intellectual and creative energy. They are places of hugely diversified activities and functions: exhibitions and demonstrations, bars and cathedrals, shops and opera houses. This work celebrates the combination of ages, races, cultures and activities, the mix of community and anonymity, familiarity and surprise, the grand spaces as well as the animation that simple pavement cafes bring to the street, the informal liveliness of the public square, the mixture of workplaces, shops and homes that make living neighbourhoods.

Although inner-city blight is slowly being addressed in a number of cities in Europe as well as abroad, great urban meeting places are still being eroded and violated by the ever-increasing intrusion and unseemly domination of the motor car. Public areas have become dangerous and polluting rather than lively and invigorating. Neighbourhoods are fragmented, citizens flee city centres in alarming numbers and the essence of a city – its human vitality – is being sucked out, leaving behind ghost towns offering only physical dereliction and social exclusion.

This book can be seen as a key element in reversing this trend. The insistence on imaginative urban design means that we can celebrate Copenhagen's renaissance as a catalyst for the many cities in Europe and abroad desperately in need of similar skills. If confirmation were needed that a well-designed city is the only sustainable form of community, then this brilliant book provides it.

London, October 2000
Richard Rogers

Introduction

For a rather long time – from the 1930s until the 1970s – nothing much happened in the field of public space and public space architecture. One explanation is the modernists' rejection of the city and public space. Another is the rapid development of car traffic and the focus on roads and transport. Finally, in Europe at any rate, the rebuilding after the Second World War and subsequent rapid urban growth meant that city planners and architects had other priorities.

However, the tide began to turn around the year 1970. Modernism began to be challenged and public debate took up the issues of urban quality and the conditions for life in the city, pollution and the car's rapid encroachment of urban streets and squares. Public space and public life were reintroduced as significant objects of architectural debate and treatment, among others. Public space architecture has been under constant development ever since and a very great number of new or renovated public spaces were created in the last quarter of the 20th century.

The object of this book is to present selected examples of public space strategies as well as projects illustrating developments in the area of public space architecture.

The architectural treatment of public space has naturally been an important starting point, but life in the city and the interplay between urban life and public space has also been emphasised. The selection and discussion of the individual cities and public spaces is influenced by this interest in the city as meeting place and public space as facilitator.

The material presented here was compiled during the years 1992-2000. The work was carried out in stages starting with an extensive search through magazines and books on the subject, followed by study trips to potentially interesting cities and public spaces. During these study visits public spaces were seen in context and data on the individual spaces, their surroundings and functions were collected.

For each of the public spaces selected, a plan of the space was drawn in a scale of 1:2,000. Maps were also drawn showing the city and the surrounding areas in comparable scales.

In selecting the cities and public spaces covered here, the objective was to come up with a representative sample that would illustrate the most important policies and design ideas underlying the work on public space. In addition to the many examples from Europe, other parts of the world also contribute attitudes and ideas developed under different political and cultural conditions.

Common to the examples here is that they are public spaces in an urban context. A few promenades are included, but the majority of the examples are squares that are new or were thoroughly renovated in the past 10 or 20 years. All are outdoor spaces designed with an urban character and treatment.

The book is divided into three parts.

Winning back public spaces: The salient features of the development of public space and public life primarily from 1975 to 2000.

9 cities and 9 public space strategies: Examples of cities that have worked towards a unified vision in their treatment of public space.

39 public spaces: 3 streets and 36 squares presented as examples.

The book can be viewed – and read – as an overall presentation of the issues or as a reference book in which ideas, projects and visions are introduced in the interests of information and – we hope – inspiration.

The Royal Danish Academy of Fine Arts
School of Architecture
November 2000
Jan Gehl & Lars Gemzøe

new public spaces
new public life

winning back public space

New city life

It is the year 2000, a summer day in the middle of Copenhagen. The city centre, once dominated by cars, has completely changed character. Pedestrian streets, pedestrian priority streets and ordinary, narrow peaceful streets form an extensive network of comfortable walking routes. The city actually invites foot traffic. The eighteen squares in the core of the city have been stripped of parking spaces and returned to the public for recreational activities. They too invite people to come and stay awhile, and to engage in other public activities that need space.

The city has created space for many different forms of human interaction. Over the past forty years, a total of 100,000 m^2 once devoted to motorised traffic have been converted to 100,000 m^2 of traffic-free city space for pedestrians. The surfaces of streets and squares have been replaced with fine stone materials, and street lighting and furniture have been refined as well. The entire city centre now has a character and an atmosphere that invite people to walk and to spend time there. The streets seem to signal: Come, you are welcome. Walk awhile, stop awhile and stay as long as you like. City space has been given a new form and a new content.

The new reclaimed people spaces are used often and used well. On this June day the streets are almost completely filled with pedestrians moving through the city at a leisurely, almost languorous pace. In fact 80% of the movement through the city centre is foot traffic. The whole of inner Copenhagen has become an area devoted to people on foot. Copenhagen has also become a place to stop and stay awhile. On this summer weekday there are between 5,000 and 6,000 Copenhageners taking advantage of the many opportunities the city offers for recreational urban activities. 1,500 seats on benches and 5,000 sidewalk cafe chairs provide ample opportunity to sit, and they are in almost constant use. Children play, young people skate by on rollerblades and

skateboards, while street musicians, artists and agitators of many kinds attract crowds to the squares. Life on the street unfolds as a colourful and varied pageant this summer day. One common trait is that a solid proportion of the activities are recreational. Another is that most of the activities are social. The city's new car-free space is used for a special form of social recreation, urban recreation, in which the opportunity to see, meet and interact with other people is a significant attraction.

This summer day in central Copenhagen speaks volumes about renewed city spaces. In addition, the pattern of the city centre is now being followed in the surrounding residential areas of the city. The conversion of streets and squares has inspired new urban patterns, which in turn have breathed new life into old neighbourhoods. Similar patterns can be found in cities throughout Europe and in other parts of the world where room has been provided for public life.

Renewed interest in public life and the city as meeting place, as it has developed over the past 30 or 40 years, has naturally led to noticeable development in urban planning and public space architecture. This development forms the central theme of the descriptions of city strategies and projects for new public spaces in the following chapters.

Traditional uses of public space: Meeting place, market-place and traffic space

Although the pattern of usage has varied in the course of history, despite differences, subtle and otherwise, public space has always served as meeting place, marketplace and traffic space. The city has always been a place for people to meet and greet each other, a place to exchange information about the city and society, a place where important events were staged: coronations, processions, feasts and festivals, town meetings and executions, to mention just a few.

The city was also a marketplace, where goods and services were offered

A summer day in Copenhagen, one of the many cities around the world to see a dramatic development in public life in step with improvements in public space.

1880

1960

1880. Copenhagen's main thoroughfare at Christmas time, depicted in a painting by Erik Henningsen reflecting the social and economic reality of the time. Of necessity, the street was a workplace, a place to sell or transport goods. The more privileged used the street for shopping and promenading, to see and be seen.

1960. The same street invaded by car traffic. Pedestrians are confined to two narrow pavements with almost no room for anything but to keep moving.

1968

2000

1968. Five years after pedestrianisation. Walking, shopping and window-shopping dominate. The social function of seeing and being seen continues to be an integral part of street life.

2000. The same street on a summer day. Six times more area is available to pedestrians. People are still in transit, but now they have other options. Many are standing, sitting or sipping refreshments at numerous outdoor cafes.

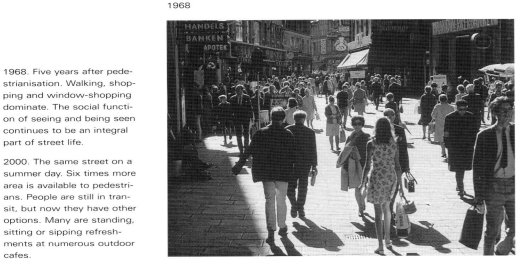

Traditionally there was a good balance between the city's functions as meeting place, marketplace and traffic space. This pattern continues in a number of well-preserved old cities, such as Venice, Italy, shown here.

Trade and traffic have completely changed character in the course of the 20th century. Cars have taken over the streets (Madrid, Spain, far left), and shopping has moved indoors (underground shopping concourse, Nagoya, Japan).

and exchanged. Finally, the city was a thoroughfare providing access to and connecting the various uses of the city. People walked about and goods were hauled from one place to another.

In the past, when most movement was conducted on foot, there was often a good balance between the three uses of the city. Pedestrians were able to walk where they needed to go, meeting, trading, talking and taking in the sights all in the same trip through town. The uses of the city were conducted simultaneously in the same public space.

However, in the 20th century, particularly in the industrialised nations, conditions for the three main uses of public space changed. New patterns of traffic, trade and communication were so radical that they interrupted centuries of tradition as to how people used the city.

Electric trams and bicycles, introduced at the end of the 19th century, gave people a wider range and allowed the city to expand significantly in area. Once cars were introduced at the beginning of the 20th century, transportation patterns changed dramatically. Particularly after the Second World War, car traffic in the city developed by leaps and bounds and the use of public space changed accordingly. Heavy car traffic does not coexist peacefully alongside the uses of the city as meeting place and marketplace. Uses that had been in balance for centuries were now in open conflict.

The city as marketplace also underwent dramatic changes in the 20th century. Trade from open booths was gradually moved to small shops along streets and squares, then to increasingly larger shops and supermarkets, and finally to giant shopping malls, usually far from the heart of the city. In those cases where shopping centres were established within the city, they closed in on themselves and were no longer part of the public arena. Trading takes place in indoor enclaves through a labyrinth of private walkways complete with small squares, bubbling fountains, muzak and air conditioning. In the process, the marketplace with its

attendant "public life" has become strictly controlled, with all activities and human interaction regulated by security guards. Quite literally, the market was taken from the public arena and moved to the private sphere. The 20th century also decisively changed the conditions for the city's use as meeting place and information exchange.

The rapid and extensive development of print and electronic news media has made it possible to provide people with an endless stream of information about the community and the wider world. No town crier needed here.

At the same time, a seemingly endless stream of opportunities for indirect communication from person to person emerged: first the telegraph, then the telephone, the cell phone, e-mail, the Internet. Individual mobility provided by cars and other forms of transportation and the development of cheap forms of long-distance travel provided new opportunities for people to meet other people.

The traditional role of the city as an important meeting place for its citizens had changed completely.

Here at the dawning of the new millennium, these massive changes in society within only a century make the vitality of public life in central Copenhagen of special interest. The many people on the streets and in the squares have chosen to be there, to walk and spend time in public spaces. Despite the many developments and changes in patterns of use, as a marketplace and meeting place the city continues to offer a significant alternative, a valuable supplement to the multitude of other options.

Current uses of public space

A look at different cities and cultural patterns in countries where communications, marketplaces and transportation have undergone radical changes in the last century gives a varied picture of the current uses of public space and the conditions for the use of the city as a public arena.

Types of information and communication channels have also undergone a major transformation.

Middle: Modern rendezvous, Oslo, Norway.

Left: Banks of public telephones, San José, Costa Rica.

Using a good measure of simplification, at this point in history it is possible to observe and describe four very different types of cities.

- The traditional city – where meeting place, marketplace and traffic continue to coexist in balance, more or less.
- The invaded city – where a single use, usually car traffic, has usurped territory at the expense of the other uses of city space.
- The abandoned city – where public space and public life have disappeared.
- The reconquered city – where strong efforts are being made to find a new, workable balance between the uses of the city as meeting place, marketplace and traffic space.

The traditional city

In the Middle Ages, towns emerged on the premise of pedestrian traffic. Streets were adapted to foot traffic and squares tailored to uses that needed space: markets, town meetings, military parades, religious processions and so on.

Even today, particularly in Europe, there are still many cities whose structure was formed during that period, and thus the centres of many European cities still have the character of the Middle Ages, as do many villages and small towns.

Isolated examples of intact medieval cities continue to function in traditional ways, with Venice as one of the best-known examples. Common to the cities and public space of that period is that they continue to be well suited for all types of pedestrian activities. The scale of these cities, the dimensions of the streets, the distribution of uses along streets and squares, the scale and detail of buildings are in harmony with human senses and opportunities for movement, and they support the comings and goings of pedestrians very directly.

In these cities throughout time, public spaces have served simultaneously as meeting place, marketplace and traffic space. In those cities in which car traffic has not been allowed to take over, we can still see modern versions of the traditional uses of public space.

The invaded city

In old cities and urban areas where car traffic has gained the upper hand, public space has inevitably changed dramatically.

Car traffic and parking have gradually usurped space in streets and squares. Not much physical space is left, and when other restrictions and irritants such as dirt, noise and visual pollution are added, it doesn't take long to impoverish city life. It becomes unpleasant and difficult to get around on foot, and spending time in public spaces is made impossible by lack of room and by environmental problems. The result in city after city is that only the most essential foot traffic battles its way between moving and parked cars, and only a severely amputated selection of other activities can be found.

Numerous studies have shown the obvious correlation between urban quality and public life.

Public spaces offering many qualities and few disadvantages inspire a broad spectrum of urban activities. Attractive walking routes and places to stop along the way encourage foot traffic which in turn promotes social and recreational activities, because people walking along become inspired to linger and enjoy the urban scene.

In impoverished public spaces, most of the social and recreational activities disappear completely, leaving only the remnants of the most utilitarian and nessesary pedestrian activities. People walk there because they have to, not because they want to.

In most of the cities besieged by cars, the quality of public space has become so problematic that people avoid the city centre altogether.

Many traditional urban spaces were designed to emphasise the city's function as meeting place. Bollards at Piazza del Campo in Siena, Italy provide psychological and practical support as well as the perfect spot for people-watching.

Prague, Czech Republic

Westport, Ireland

Riyadh, Saudi Arabia

Istanbul, Turkey

Naples, Italy

Above: The invaded city. Urban life is reduced drastically – or made completely impossible – as car traffic invades cities.

Right, overleaf: There are other forms of invasion, too, such as reducing the variety of urban functions. Shown here, large office blocks in Stockholm, Sweden.

The abandoned city

Where urban tradition is weaker and car culture has had more time to develop without major constraints from urban planning, a new type of city develops. This city has no historical model, because for the first time in history pedestrian traffic has been made impossible or superfluous, and many of the other activities traditionally tied to foot traffic in public spaces have disappeared completely. Public life in public places is gone. There are many cities of this type in many places, although predominately in North America. City centres are a sea of asphalt with parking places marking off the space between buildings. Walking is impossible and would also be unreasonable. Distances are too great and the environments an intrepid pedestrian might encounter on his way would be ugly, dirty and possibly dangerous. Such cities are not intended for walking. Sidewalks have disappeared in the city centres as well as residential areas, and all the uses of the city have gradually been adapted to serve the motorist. Transportation and life itself are totally dependent on the car in a drive-in culture. It is difficult to describe the total consequences of this type of urban policy. However, it is important to point out that heavy dependency on the automobile means that children too young to drive, the elderly who are too old to drive and the handicapped who are physically prevented from driving are consigned to a life of being transported everywhere by others. Indeed, for young people life doesn't really start until the day they turn 16 and acquire their driving license!

People shop from drive-in stores along car-filled streets, by and large requiring the driver to drive and re-park at each destination. The alternative is to shop in large shopping centres outside the cities. And only in these centres is it still possible to walk both from the car park to the centre and inside on the walkways of the covered centre itself.

As a countermeasure to the regional shopping centres and as a strategy for maintaining turnover and uses of the city centre, numerous cities

In a historical perspective, the abandoned city is new. Walking is impossible or superfluous and public life in public space no longer exists.

Top: The city centre as car park, Spokane, Wa. USA

Middle: Empty street scene, Clarksdale, Miss. USA

Right: Street scene, Atlanta, Ga. USA

have experimented with new forms of shopping environments adapted to car culture.

In some cities shops have been moved indoors into atriums and shopping arcades within the city centre itself. The Eaton Centre in Toronto is one example.

Other cities such as Calgary, Winnipeg, Minneapolis and Atlanta have built skywalks, systems of pedestrian bridges running one or two storeys above street level and connecting shops placed strategically inside the buildings of the city centre. Here pedestrians are lifted up a storey and can move about indoors from building to building, protected from the weather and free from streets and other public space.

A third category of centrally located, private shopping environment is "the underground city" as the phenomenon is known in Montreal and Toronto in Canada, as well as in cities such as Sapporo, Nagoya and Osaka in Japan. These cities, often in connection with underground metro stations, have set up a network of shopping centres and walkways that connect the lower storeys of buildings in the city centre.

Common to all of these types of shopping centres is that they are private and closed outside office hours, and that both pedestrian activities and other city activities are subject to heavy restrictions conditional on the commercial character of the centres. There is no room for versatility, humour and democracy on the agenda of these very standardised, modern shopping centres.

An interesting public health problem has developed in these cities where it is virtually impossible to walk or bicycle as a natural part of daily routine. Many of the urban inhabitants are overweight and in poor physical condition. Some of them try to combat the problem by jogging during their lunch breaks or spending time in fitness centres or working out on some of the many exercise machines designed by the fitness industry to fill this need.

For other segments of the population, who have neither the opportunity nor the motivation to engage in fitness activities, the problem literally grows larger and larger. Indeed, doing away with pedestrian traffic and public space – and public life to a great extent – has many direct and indirect consequences.

New problems arise when people no longer walk for daily exercise.

Above: Lunch-time fitness with landscape painting on the back wall. IT company, Silicon Valley, Ca. USA.

Right: Park-n-Sweat structure with seven storeys of parking and a two-storey fitness centre, Atlanta, Ga. USA.

The reconquered city

Over the past 30 to 40 years, interest in public spaces and public life has begun to grow again, often as a direct reaction to the increasingly poorer conditions for both, and in many cities efforts are now being made to give pedestrians and urban life better odds.

Paradoxically enough, one important source of inspiration came from shopping malls, particularly in the USA. Already in the 1920s when the first malls were built, it was clear that customers had to be lured out of their cars and into car-free shopping streets in order to have the peace of mind to concentrate on shopping. Some of the earliest pedestrian areas in Europe such as Lijnbahn, built in war-torn Rotterdam in the 1950s, and the rebuilding of many German cities in the same period, had this same starting point. Many of the other pedestrian areas established in the 1960s and 1970s throughout Europe, including the pedestrian street in mid-Copenhagen from 1962, were also based primarily on this commercial concept. While true that pedestrian streets made it easier for people to get about downtown, the primary purpose of having them was to get people to shop.

The idea of using public space as social and recreational space grew gradually and was reinforced during the decades that followed. Jane Jacob's description of the development in American cities in her book "The Death and Life of Great American Cities", published in 1961, had major impact. Many American and European researchers also contributed by pointing out the importance of varied forms of public life in the public spaces of the city. The connection between city quality and the extent and character of city life was also documented during this same period.

Particularly in Europe, tradition was a third and very important source of inspiration. Many European cities continued to carry on a lively tradition of using public spaces for social and recreational activities. Throughout this period, the 1960s and 1970s, more and more pedestrian streets,

areas and peaceful squares were established in European cities. Conditions for pedestrians were also gradually improved in many of the other streets in major cities. Sidewalks were widened and enhanced with street furniture, flowers and trees.

An important turning point for the traffic situation in cities was the oil crisis starting in 1973. The break in traffic expansion led to planned efforts to limit the encroachment of cars in the cities as well as other measures to ensure a better balance between motorists and other forms of transport. Interest in bicycling and public transportation grew accordingly. Throughout this whole period, the concepts for new public spaces expanded. Once confined to narrow commercial interests, concepts now had a considerably broader focus: creating space and conditions for walking under reasonable provisions and ensuring development opportunities for social and recreational urban activities.

Although many cities in Germany and Scandinavia pioneered efforts to push back cars from the city centres and create more peaceful conditions for pedestrians, it was in Barcelona, starting in about 1980, that a broader concept of public spaces was formulated in a co-ordinated public space policy. In the course of 50 years, all city space had been conquered by cars. Now the city was fighting back, both physically and culturally. It was also in Barcelona that the concept of "the reconquered city" was born. In terms of both idea and specific architectural formulation, public space policy in Barcelona came to play a major role in further developments. What happened in Barcelona was the starting point for a new, intense period in the last 20 years of the 20th century, in which increasingly more good urban spaces were created or renewed, in order to ensure good public space for new types of public life.

If we are looking for development patterns in the most recent decades, it is clear that several European cities left their mark. In terms of policy, the Dutch, German and Scandinavian cities were among the first to experiment

New ideas are adopted to regain lost public space.

Shown here: In Stockholm, Sweden new housing has been built on top of existing multi-storey car parks. Empty streets dominated by cars and concrete are changed to narrow streets lined by housing and shops.

with new types of city space. More recently, many cities in central and southern Europe have followed suit.

The policy of pushing back cars and giving urban life better conditions continues to be a European phenomenon primarily, but it is interesting to note that corresponding urban policy strategies can now be found in cities in North and South America, Asia and Australia. Precisely because of what has happened in other regions on these continents, the efforts made in Portland, Oregon and Curitiba, Brazil are remarkable, and show that we can no longer refer to public space strategies as being solely a European phenomenon.

Every part of the world has desolate, invaded and abandoned cities, and all over the world there are cities that have fought back by inviting inhabitants to return and use public space.

The marked differences from city to city within the same cultural circles underline another interesting common trait, namely that most urban improvements are carried out or at least initiated by visionary individuals or groups. It can be a mayor, a city architect, a city council, a political party or inspirational co-operation between consultants, politicians and grassroots movements, but common to the cities that have recaptured public space is visionary, targeted urban policies.

Typically, various topics are combined in these urban visions, such as traffic safety, changes in traffic patterns, public health, a reduction in resource consumption, a reduction in noise and pollution – and efforts to strengthen the role of the city as a democratic forum. Where visions and political will go hand in hand to meet a number of these objectives, it is clear that cities actually do become better places in which to live and spend time.

Lost public space is being regained and new urban spaces established all over the world due to the desire for a better balance between the functions of the city as marketplace, meeting place and traffic space.

Above: Centre Pompidou, Paris, France.

Below from left: New public space in Seattle, Wa. USA. Public space along the reopened waterway in Århus, Denmark. Renovated pedestrian street, San Jóse, Costa Rica.

New public spaces for new public life

Although this book on new city spaces and public life starts out one summer day in the centre of Copenhagen, it is just one of many cities in which urban policy initiatives have raised urban quality. Traffic, noise and pollution have been reduced, foot traffic and bicycle traffic have been reinforced. Public life has blossomed on the streets and squares of the city in a way not seen 20 or 30 years ago, certainly not in the form it has today, which is not even a new version of an older urban tradition, but a truly new phenomenon. The overwhelming interest in and backing for the new public life in public spaces is certainly thought provoking.

In a society in which increasingly more of daily life takes place in the private sphere – in private homes, at private computers, in private cars, at private workplaces and in strictly controlled and privatised shopping centres – there are clear signs that the city and city spaces have been given a new and influential role as public space and forum.

In contrast to the many indirect communications and the many widespread and private spaces, the opportunity for people to use their senses and interact directly with their surroundings is becoming extremely attractive. The information society is providing new meaning and significance to the city as meeting place.

It is these new public spaces and public life that are the main theme for the treatment of cities and public spaces in this book.

With daily life increasingly privatised and indirect communication growing by leaps and bounds, the need for public life in public space is growing. Here people can experience direct contact with other people and the society of which we are a part. Here they can see things for themselves, experience, participate and feel a sense of community.

Examples shown from France, USA, Norway, Brazil and Denmark.

New life in the city. A summer day at Sankt
Hans Torv, a new urban square in Nørrebro,
Copenhagen, Denmark.

barcelona
lyon
strasbourg
freiburg
copenhagen
portland
curitiba
cordoba
melbourne

**9 cities
9 public space strategies**

9 cities – 9 public space strategies: Introduction

In most cases when existing public space is renovated or new public spaces established, designs are made for individual projects. Numerous very interesting designs have resulted from these efforts, and several such examples are presented later in this book.

With this in mind, special interest must be given to cities where efforts have been made to develop unified public space policies and to see the individual public space projects in a larger context.

Naturally, the goals, priorities and extent of measures taken vary from city to city, just as different elements are emphasised: architectural unity, conditions for pedestrian traffic, recreational opportunities or the desire to improve the traffic situation generally, for example.

Most interesting of all are the visions that constitutes a combined strategy aimed at improving overall urban quality by including social, functional, and ecological aspects as well as traffic concerns and architectural considerations.

In order to illustrate various ways of working with comprehensive policies for public spaces, nine cities from different parts of the world have been selected.

They span a wide range of goals and priorities. Public space strategy in some of the cities comprises only one or two elements, while other cities have taken on imaginative and extensive combinations of sectors in their work to develop a unified public space policy.

Within this wide category, emphasis has been placed on cities with versatile, co-ordinated public space policies including guidelines for public space, public life, traffic policies and architectural treatment. Cities successful in improving the conditions for public life and thus the function of the city as meeting place have been of special interest in connection with the emphasis of this book.

In making the selection, priority was also given to cities concerned with sustainability issues as evidenced by programs for limiting private car traffic and encouraging energy-saving forms of transport. It is interesting that there is often a close connection between these aims. Cities with strategies to reduce car traffic or to promote architectural quality or sustainability often prove to be cities that offer the best conditions for pedestrians and public life.

A comparison of the nine cities shows considerable differences with respect to the strategies adopted.

Work on specific points throughout the city as opposed to larger concentrated areas represents two very different starting points. In the first case localities of special importance are selected and public spaces throughout the city are renovated successfully to become attractive oases in the cityscape. In many ways, the public space strategy followed in Barcelona represents this strategy.

In other cases, the city aims at broader treatment of large connected urban areas, dealing with many aspects together. The renovation of the public spaces in the centre of Copenhagen is an example of this strategy. The issue of city centre versus peripheral areas is another important aspect illustrated in the selected examples. In some cities, urban policy narrowly targets only the inner city, while other cities take a broader view of the inner city as well as many urban neighbourhoods outside the city centre.

Seen together the nine cities presented on the following pages may serve to provide an overview of current thinking about public space strategies and public space visions.

The structure in each of the nine cities is illustrated by a map in a scale of 1:20,000. The map shows a 2.2 x 2.2 kilometre section of the city centre, and describes dimensions and patterns. Selected elements characteristic of the public space strategy of the individual cities are marked.

Barcelona

Large Southern European city that adopted targeted measures to establish fine public spaces for recreational and social activities in all parts of the city. Innovative architecture is the hallmark of the many projects.

Lyon

Medium-size European city that concentrated its resources to breathe new life into a large number of city spaces in the inner city as well as outlying quarters. Precise urban design guidelines for managing the architectural elements is key.

Strasbourg

A new political role inspired the implementation of a combined traffic and public space policy. City life, pedestrians, bicyclists and pubic transport are strengthened and car traffic limited.

Freiburg

For decades, this small European city has had a targeted policy to improve conditions for pedestrians, bicyclists and public transport. Carefully considered architectural elements connect the various city spaces.

Copenhagen

Better public spaces, more life in the city, more bicyclists and less car traffic – implemented gradually over four decades. Systematic studies show a dramatic development in urban life.

Portland

A comprehensive city policy benefited pedestrians with wide sidewalks, good public spaces and parks and new forms of public transport in this North American city.

Curitiba

For three decades this Brazilian city has made impressive strides to reinforce the development of a sustainable city with good conditions for public transport and life in public spaces.

Cordoba

Argentine city with a traditional grid street pattern. The pedestrian streets, squares and parks in the heart of the city have been treated on the basis of a unified, imaginative architectural vision.

Melbourne

Australian city with a traditional grid street pattern attesting to its colonial past. Major efforts were made to maintain and strengthen pedestrian traffic and the vitality of the streets of the inner city.

The nine cities presented in the following work with strategies that often involve initiatives and projects in several sectors. Rather than present the cities according to the content and elements of their strategies, we decided on a regional breakdown starting with Barcelona and the other European cities from south to north, followed by cities in North and South America and then Australia.

Barcelona

Spain

Visionary thinking and pioneering public space policy

For the past two decades, Barcelona has been the most important source of inspiration for architects, landscape architects, urban planners and politicians who work with public spaces. Nowhere else in the world can the viewer see in one and the same city so many different examples of new parks and squares and so much exuberance and experimentation in their design.

Barcelona has been both radical and imaginative in implementing public space policy. In only a decade, several hundred new parks, squares and promenades were created by tearing down dilapidated apartment buildings, warehouses and factories, as well as by reno-vating existing squares and regulating traffic to benefit pedestrians.

N

100 200 300 400 500 metres

1:20,000

Above: Map showing the old city centre plus part of the harbour and adjacent neigh-bourhoods. New public spaces created between 1980-2000 in the area covered by the map are shown. The location of Barce-lona's famous promenade, La Rambla, is also shown.

Aerial photo of Barcelona from the east. The picture gives an indication of the
extent of the city and its dense building structure. Foreground: the harbour and
old city centre. Behind them are the distinctive city blocks designed by Idelfonso
Cerda and traversed by large diagonals. Urban renewal in all parts of the city is
characteristic of public space policy in Barcelona.

The city

Barcelona is a vibrant city of almost 3 million people on the coast of the Mediterranean in the Catalonian region of Northeast Spain. The city centre is dense and compact, reflecting centuries of population growth within the confines of city walls and ramparts, as in many other old European cities. Compact quarters interlaced by narrow streets lined by tall buildings border each side of the Rambla, which connects the harbour with Plaça Catalunya. Skirting the old city is a new one that mushroomed at the end of the last century when the old city walls were torn down. The new city was built according to a new and radical plan by Idelfonso Cerda. Designed as a large grid with wide thoroughfares connecting to the old city, new neighbourhoods grew up outside the limits of the old walled city. The grid is traversed by a couple of wide diagonal boulevards. The plan was envisioned as the basis for building a new green and open city designed as quadratic urban blocks with chamfered corners that create a square at every street intersection. The intention was less density and wider streets than in the old part of the city.

Today the new part of the city is very dense, and on the whole, Barcelona is one of the most densely built cities in Europe. Under Franco's long dictatorship, the city was woefully neglected and large urban areas sprang up on the outskirts of the city without any real form of planning, bringing with them numerous problems with traffic and infrastructure generally.

Public space policy

With the election in 1979, the first free election since the end of the Spanish Civil War in 1939, a new government led by the Socialists came into power. The newly won democratic freedom led to an avalanche of initiatives on all fronts, and liberated a generation of architects who had been straitjacketed by the dictatorship – architects who had not been willing to compromise their work by co-operating with the regime. Under Franco, the Catalonians had been repressed both politically and linguistically.

The new city government appointed one of the region's leading architects, Oriol Bohigas, head of the school of architecture, as the new city counsellor for urban design, a position that gave him the opportunity to formulate and inspire others to adopt a new public space policy. The city government wanted to show the citizens of Barcelona some immediate improvements, things that could be done here and now, so Bohigas developed a policy that emphasised projects rather than plans. Planning was changed from the traditional long-term planning of function and area, where the initiative for implementation is largely dependent on the investment interest of private industry, to an active city policy, in which the public sector initiated renewal by designing dozens of new public spaces, parks and squares.

Architecture was made one of the main instruments of urban policy, and numerous new public spaces were created. Every quarter was to have its own "living room" and every district its park, where people could meet and talk and children could play.

Characteristic of Barcelona's urban policy is that public spaces spring from the need for room for people to gather in true democratic tradition, as well as ample space for pedestrians. On the whole, public spaces were created by pulling down dilapidated apartment buildings or abandoned factories, and only to a small extent by limiting the area already devoted to motorised traffic. A number of squares in the city centre were renovated in conjunction with building underground parking areas, but this was not characteristic of the policy.

In the old city centre, several of the new squares were created by tearing down existing buildings to create space for the new meeting places in the very dense core of the city. On the outskirts, new meeting places were created under the banner "to put a face on the faceless". Here improve-

Far left: With Gaudí's Casa Mila in the background, Passeig de Grácia is one of the wide boulevards in the Eixample quarter.

Middle: The narrow streets and dense building in the old city centre, Ciutat Vella.

Left: La Rambla in the centre of Barcelona is the city's major pedestrian street.

ments were aimed at large sprawling areas that had sprung up in the 1960s and lacked identity and public space. The new policy, which was introduced under the first mayor after Franco's dictatorship, Narcis Serra, made fast, visible improvements for local areas in all parts of the city. At the same time, the improvements had a contagious effect on private initiatives, for example, urban renewal and renovation of the many dilapidated buildings. Pasqual Maragall, elected mayor in 1982, expressed the underlying philosophy of the policy like this: "We want to re-create the lost dignity of the urban landscape and to stimulate and direct the energy of the marketplace."

The city rose again like the proverbial Phoenix during the process, also providing the platform for the giant Olympic projects that became the economic locomotive for the further planning of the entire city.

Architecture and sculpture have played a key role in the design of Barcelona's public face. New parks and squares were created under the motto: "Move museums into the street." Essentially all new public spaces boast a work of art by internationally famous artists. The unique characteristics of each square were thus emphasised by the design of the space itself, as well as by the individual works of art, giving each quarter a public platform for every occasion.

Almost all of the new projects involved co-operation between artists and architects. One example of sculpture that is an integral part of design is Plaça de la Palmera, where Richard Serra's curving walls divide the dual character of the square. Another example is Via Julia, where the large "lighthouse" is the focus of the square. In several parks, sculptures are designed to appeal to play and climbing, such as Parc de l'Estació del Nord, which has a huge smooth ceramic sculpture, and Parc de l'Espanya Industrial, which features a giant iron dragon, designed so that children can slide on it.

The first projects from the end of the 1970s and beginning of the 1980s were marked by their placement in the old city, and they reflect respect for tradition. With their traditional materials and furnishings, some of these squares look as if they have been there for hundreds of years. For example, Plaça Reial, which is an old square, has been renovated with a new pavement, while Plaça de la Mercè is a new space created by tearing down existing buildings.

The squares and parks that lie outside the old city centre are different. Here we can see experimentation with forms of expression, and the spaces look very contemporary in their design, furniture and choice of materials. Plaça dels Països Catalans, the square in front of Sants train station, is one of the many public spaces that break with tradition and the conventions concerning how a square should look.

Oriol Bohigas handpicked several architects to carry out the first experiments in designing new city spaces. They were given the opportunity to work in a field in which they had no previous experience, but the refined Catalan tradition of concern for detail and choice of materials was good ballast.

In a decade, their experimentation made Barcelona an undisputed leading laboratory in the design of city spaces in terms of imagination, variation and volume of solutions. In no other city is it possible to see such a large number of innovative designs for public space. Barcelona's architects have been nothing short of pioneers in elevating public space to the level of an independent architectural field, after this discipline had all but disappeared under the influence of modernism.

Urban design office

A special office, Servei de Projectes Urbans, was set up to work with public spaces. The office is responsible for the design of the many projects and the co-ordination of the many bodies that take part in the realisation of new city spaces in the ten districts into which the city is divided. Each

The "museums of the street".

Right: Via Julia, the sculptural "lighthouse" by Antoni Roselló.

Middle: Plaça de la Palmera with two curved walls by Richard Serra.

Far right: Parc de l'Estació del Nord, ceramic sculpture by Beverly Pepper.

Very few standard elements were used to furnish Barcelona's urban spaces. Inventory and lighting fixtures were often designed for the individual sites.

Right: Jardí de la Villa Cecília.

Middle: Barcelona's waterfront.

Far right: Rambla de Prim.

Above: Plaça Reial, a classic urban space, underwent respectful renovation, primarily of the floor.

Left: Renovation of the area in front of Barcelona's train station created a contemporary, pioneering public space, Plaça dels Països Catalans.

district has a team of architects who hold meetings and discussions with local residents and independently handle the projects in their district. In addition to the famous tried-and-true architects, many young architects have been able to carry out their projects in Barcelona. Architecture students are recruited to work at the urban design office, for example, by holding design contests for students and offering them a job working in their field. A visit to the urban design office at the end of the 1980s showed that this enthusiastic workplace had completed between 300-400 projects of all sizes. A look at one of the many small guidebooks published by the urban design office in the same decade shows that a surprising number of different architects and artists had the opportunity to make their contribution to the varied and innovative picture presented by the many public spaces. More than 90 architects, either alone or in teams, are mentioned as responsible for the execution of the 55 streets, parks and squares described in the guidebook. The design of space from the overall level to the tiniest detail on the basis of strong ideas and site - specific solutions – these are the special contributions Barcelona has made to planning public spaces in the 1980s.

With the major projects leading up to the Olympic Summer Games in 1992, several offices became involved in the work at the regional level. Afterwards, the urban design office continued to be responsible for the co-ordination of new projects, but private architect firms do much of the actual designing.

In total Barcelona's public spaces comprise an impressive variation of different designs of lighting, furniture and surfaces. There is no such thing as a limited standard set of materials and urban idioms. On the contrary, there is strong emphasis on designing each individual space as an independent site with its own identity. Often a bench or lighting fixture has been designed for one site exclusively, although with time a number of elements have been adopted for use elsewhere. One example is the

beautiful flower-like light fixture that was designed for Jardí de la Villa Cecília, but can now be seen in the new urban neighbourhood built originally for the Olympic Village. One possible downside to this wealth of solutions is the considerable maintenance problem encountered at many sites later on, worsened to some extent by the use of many different materials, details and types of furniture.

Types of public spaces

Along with the expanse and wealth of variety, there are a number of basic traits that make it possible to define a few main types among the many newly renovated city spaces.

A number of squares have the character of "stone rooms" and they often serve as urban living rooms and meeting places. These rather hard spaces feature stone surfaces and furniture, occasionally softened by trees. Examples are several new squares created by tearing down dilapidated buildings: Plaça de la Mercè, Plaça de Sant Cugat, Fossar de les Moreres, Plaça d'Escudellers-Arenes-Arai. Other examples are renovations of existing squares such as Plaça Reial, Plaça de l'Àngel and Plaça del Sol, or squares that have changed character from traffic space to pedestrian square, such as Plaça de les Basses de Sant Pere, Plaça de Navas and the large square in front of the train station, Plaça dels Països Catalans.

Another softer public space could be called a "gravel square", with focus on a place to rest or play, often with an area of gravel as the focal element. Examples of this type are Jardí de la Indústria and Plaça de la Hispanitat, but other squares such as Plaça de General Moragues also have a gravelled area as one of the main elements. A number of new parks or "urban oases" function as large recreational urban parks dispersed throughout the urban districts of the city. An "oasis" is a combination type of park with a large variety of elements and spaces and the opportunity for activity as well as passivity. Characteristic of most of them is a large green

Far left: Fossar de les Moreres is a small square with a floor of red bricks, created as an interval in the dense heart of the city by tearing down a block of buildings.

Left: The benches along the lengthy stone floor of Parc Miró are an integral part of the design of the square.

Promenades. Aviguda D'Icaria (left) and Via Julia (far left) are examples of new interpretations of the Rambla motif.

Below: Oases. Parc de la Pegaso on the left and Parc de l'Espanya Industrial on the right are new interpretations of an urban park.

landscape element, often with gravelled areas and large surfaces of stone. Water, in the form of small ponds, fountains or waterfalls, often serves as a dividing element between gravelled surfaces and green landscapes. Examples are: Parc del Clot, Parc de Joan Miró, Parc de la Pegaso, Plaça de Sóller and Parc de l'Espanya Industrial.

Another type of space is the promenades, where places to walk as well as to sit, rest or play have been set in the midst of a lively boulevard. They are often new interpretations of the Rambla motif, where both hard and soft traffic coexist in the same space. Examples include direct interpretation of the Rambla such as Avinguda D'Icaria, Avinguda de Gaudí, and more compact types such as Via Júlia, Passeig de Picasso, and the harbour park, Moll de Bosch i Alsina, which contains an unorthodox juxtaposition of linear traffic and stationary elements. In addition to these Rambla types, which combine car traffic, walking and recreational activities, are a number of pedestrian streets of more traditional design.

The harbour front in Barcelona is part of the total picture of public spaces and contains many good design examples of the city's meeting with water. Mastery of large surfaces and edge details offers many fine solutions, as seen in Passeig National – Moll de la Barceloneta.

City spaces from Barcelona featured in the collection of projects:

Above: Afternoon at Plaça del Sol, one of the many new "living rooms" in the city.

Far left: Wheelchair access is a recurring theme throughout Barcelona. The renovation of the city's pavements includes ramps made of good stone materials.

Left and middle: There are fine examples of precise transitions between various materials along the waterfront. The examples here are from Passeig National – Moll de la Barceloneta.

Lyon

France

Poetic, coordinated and social public space policy

In only a few years, the city of Lyon has renovated numerous of its public spaces on the basis of a cohesive policy formulated in 1989. The political will to make comprehensive changes existed along with the conviction that not only the centre of the city but the entire city was involved, both socially and architecturally. The objective has been a better city for all or "a city for people", as it has been formulated. In less than a decade, several hundred urban improvement projects have been carried out to renovate outdoor areas between the large residential blocks of the suburbs, extending to the renovation of the city's main streets and squares. Characteristic of the public space policy in Lyon is work with traffic policy, which has involved creating a large number of parking spaces under the many newly renovated squares, and the use of a fixed set of furnishings and materials.

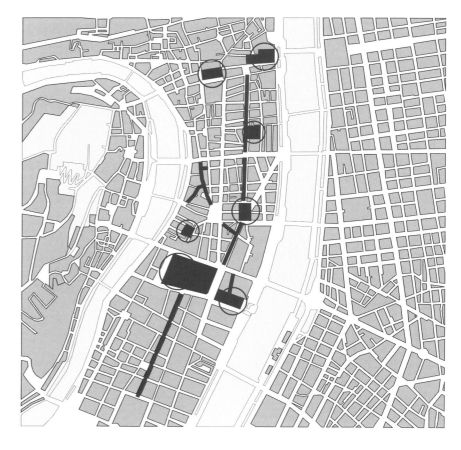

N

100 200 300 400 500 metres

1:20,000

Above: Map of the city centre between the Saône and Rhône rivers. The network of car-free and pedestrian priority streets and squares established since 1990 are shown. Circles indicate the many car parks built underneath city squares.

Aerial photo of Lyon seen from the south. In the middle is the city centre between the Rhône and Saône rivers. Public space policy includes renovation in all parts of the city, although with emphasis on inner-city areas.

The city

Greater Lyon, which lies at the meeting of the Rhône and Saône rivers, is the third largest city in France, with a population of more than 1.3 million. The old city with its crooked streets lies on the hills of the west bank of the Saône, which also contains the ruins of the Roman city of Lugduna, once an important trading hub. The city's commercial streets and cultural institutions lie on the flat peninsula between the Rhône and Saône rivers in the city centre built in the 1600s and 1700s. The city has since grown towards the north and east, where its large industrial, residential and public housing areas lie.

Public space policy

Work with the new public space policy started in the late 1980s, when City Councilman Henry Chabert in co-operation with the architect Jean Pierre Charbonneau formulated a new policy to solve the many problems the city had encountered. Problems consisted in part of strongly increased traffic in the city centre up through the 1970s and 1980s, deteriorating public space as well as massive physical and social problems in the extensive housing areas of the suburbs from the 1960s and 1970s.

In addition to the many finely designed squares, which are the visible result of the public space policy, the social considerations made in the process are an interesting aspect of Lyon's urban policy. The city council wanted to re-establish the trust in local rule for all citizens, so projects were balanced between work on the inner city and work in the suburbs. The policy has been a clear signal to inhabitants that everyone is equal and that no one gives greater priority to the city centre at the expense of the needy residential areas of the suburbs.

The desire for balance is also clearly emphasised by the fact that the same architect often designs one project in the inner city and one in the suburbs.

A green plan, a blue plan and a lighting plan

Great preparation went into the planning and the city's spatial qualities, the buildings and types of space in the individual quarters and landscape features were analysed and emphasised. These main characteristics have been made part of the basis for the various types of plans with changing themes that cover the entire urban area.

Lyon has worked with a "green plan" that comprises the public spaces and a "blue plan" that operates with the city's relations to water, particularly the banks of the Rhône and Saône rivers, which run through and define the city's central areas. Finally the city also worked on a "lighting plan" that set out guidelines for overall artistic and functional lighting of streets, squares, buildings and special urban elements such as the bridges and banks of the rivers as well as selected historical monuments. Work is ongoing to light the main street of the city, Rue de la République, with a course of facade lighting that emphasises the central importance of public space while giving pedestrians soft, functional lighting reflected by the facades. The plan is being carried out gradually in step as building owners pay to have the lighting fixtures installed, after which they are run and maintained by the municipality.

Cars and pedestrians

An important aspect of public space policy has been to push cars out of the central city. One important link in the renovation process was to establish numerous underground car parks many storeys under the newly renovated squares. The idea has been to remove parking from the surface and bury it deep, so that the city could once again be a city for people rather than cars.

The design concepts for the parking policy in the "underworld" have been just as ambitious as the quality standard set for the surface of the city. Entrances to the car parks are as a rule placed in the buildings along

Far left: Special illumination of the city bridges and important sights along the river.

Middle: Along Rue de la République the idea is to highlight the streetscape with overall facade lighting. The plan is carried out gradually as building owners pay to have the light fixtures mounted, after which maintenance is taken over by the municipality.

Left: Lyon's lighting policy includes special illumination of the city's monuments. Shown here, the opera house.

the squares or designed to be airy and spacious. Surprising effects have been used in several places, such as at Place des Célestins. Here a periscope mounted on the square, designed by artist Daniel Buren with his characteristic black and white stripes, offers an almost surrealistic look into the beautiful winding ramp of the underground, which is reflected back by the giant rotating mirror deep underground. Thus the car parks are an experience in themselves. It has also been important to make underground parking attractive and to remove the feeling of insecurity that often goes with underground parking. The entrances and exits have been very carefully designed, often with glass shields, so that they do not disrupt the streetscape. Altogether, the city of Lyon offers 12,000 inner-city parking spaces, which is a rather large parking capacity and means heavy car traffic in the areas around the city core. To compare, the centre of Copenhagen, a city the size of Lyon, has only 3,100 parking spaces and correspondingly limited traffic pressure in the areas surrounding the city centre.

Local influence, political and technical management

The actual implementation of the public space policy is managed by a project group, Group de Pilotage Espaces Public, a political committee headed up by Councilman H. Chabert. The committee comprises all of the involved parties in co-operation across the lines of the usual trade unions and public bodies such as the social sector, the highway department and the park department. The political committee meets once or twice a month, but has a corresponding interdisciplinary committee of technicians, Groupe Technique de Suivi, which reports to it and meets once a week to ensure technical co-ordination and project preparation.

Projects are started untraditionaly by inviting an author or a poet to interpret the spirit of the site and describe its life, character and special features. This description is an important part of the whole project. Not until

Above: Beneath the quiet public spaces above ground lie deep underground car parks, which are often an experience in themselves. Looking into the subterranean depths of Place des Célestins reveals a fascinating swirling ramp reflected by a giant rotating mirror.

Right: Place des Célestins, which provides a surprising view of the underground car park from a black-and-white striped periscope in the middle of the square. The periscope and reflected car-park ramp are part of artist Daniel Buren's sculpture project, "Sens dessus-dessous."

the project has had public input is the design itself turned over to a team of designers and technicians from the private sector for implementation. Residents are involved in the process to a great extent, particularly through town meetings and project exhibitions. For the most complicated projects such as the renovation of the central shopping street, Rue de la République, more than a hundred meetings were held with the involved parties, such as residents, building owners, shop owners, etc.

Fixed set of furnishings and materials

The public space policy also contains fixed materials and types of inventory used in various connections throughout the city. The same benches and lighting fixtures of high quality can be found in a renovated residential area in the suburbs and in the centre of the city. This provides a holistic effect, simplifies maintenance and makes the desired point that the various parts of the city have been given equal priority.

Many different architects, landscape architects and artists are involved in designing the various outdoor spaces of the city, so that the standardisation of materials and certain inventory has not led to standard solutions. Part of city management policy is making decisions about surfacing and the character of stone materials, for example a warm light sandstone and a fine light granite are used to connect surfaces in a number of the squares in the city centre.

Coloured concrete in harmony with the stone materials is also used.

Bright green grass surfaces that meet red or ochre coloured gravel surfaces edged by one of the stone materials mentioned above are repeated, giving the squares a special Lyon "image", while allowing each square to have its own character.

Springs and fountains are also characteristic of several of the squares in the inner city.

With its many small geysers of water over most of the surface, Place des

Jean-Michel Wilmotte designed the furnishings for Lyon, which are found throughout the renovated public spaces in the city centre as well as the suburbs.

Above: Cité Jardins de Gerland in a renovated housing area outside the city centre (top), and Place de la Bourse in the city centre (bottom).

Right: Rue de la République has become the dignified pedestrian axis of the city, its status underscored by elegant granite "runners".

Terreaux, which was designed for an architectural competition, provides a unique magical sound and light effect both day and night. The large open surface of the square with its masses of people walking between the many bursts of water has a completely different character than the intimate, green space of Place de la Bourse, not far away. It is so densely planted and contains so many pots of boxwood that the city almost disappears behind all the greenery.

Different again are the elegant granite "runners" through Rue de la République, which has once again become the city's dignified pedestrian access cutting through the middle of the city, now that the cars have been removed. The street is a key element in the extensive lighting plan and the effect is very powerful at night with almost all facades lit the full length of the street.

Place de la République with its distinctive fountain is a very welcome invitation to people to take a break and enjoy the play of the water. Or there is Place Antonin Poncet, which with its red gravel and raised green grassy areas creates a connection and a view all the way to the Rhône River, cutting across the varied stream of traffic along the riverbank. Renovation of the residential areas in the suburbs has been designed in the same way, with a variation of public spaces and meeting places that used to be anonymous leftover space between housing complexes.

Public spaces from Lyon featured in the collection of projects:
Place des Terreaux: p.156
Place de la Bourse: p.162
Place Charles Hernu: p.166

Above: Place Antonin Poncet and its impressive fountain connect the city to water across the heavily trafficked road along the riverbank.

Left: A lively fountain dominates Place de la République. Nozzles along the sides send jets of water into the centre of the pool. The cascading water completely drowns out the sound of the cars crossing the square at a snail's pace. Naturally, the jets of water in varying strengths are a big temptation to children.

Strasbourg

France

The renovation of public space and public transport for a new European capital

In only a decade starting in 1990, Strasbourg has carried out an extensive urban renewal project. The conditions for city life, bicyclists and public transport have been improved dramatically, while car traffic has been markedly reduced in the city centre. A linear public space policy introduced an elegant new tram line, which inspired the renovation of squares, streets and roads along its route. Constructing the 12.6-kilometre line literally paved the way for public space improvements both in the centre and on the outskirts of the city. The changes in public space and traffic have been a great success, and a new tram line was inaugurated in November 2000, doubling the length of tracks laid.

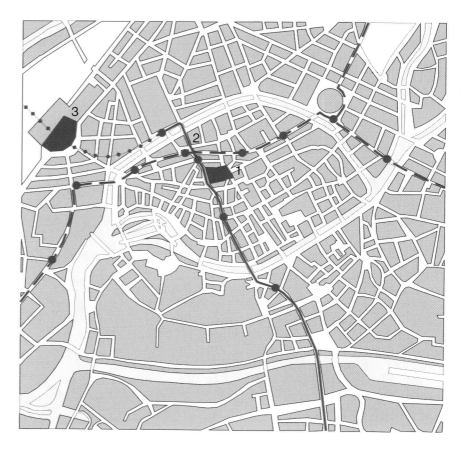

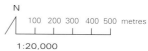

N

100 200 300 400 500 metres

1:20,000

Above: Map of the city centre and some of the outlying area. The routes and stops for the new tram lines that have served as the starting point for the renovation of city space are indicated. The solid line shows the route of Line A (inaugurated in 1994), which runs underneath the railway station (this part of the route is shown by a string of diamonds). A dotted line shows the route of Line B (inaugurated in November 2000). The location of the renovated squares is also shown: Place Kléber (1), Place de l'Homme de Fer (2) and Place de la Gare (3).

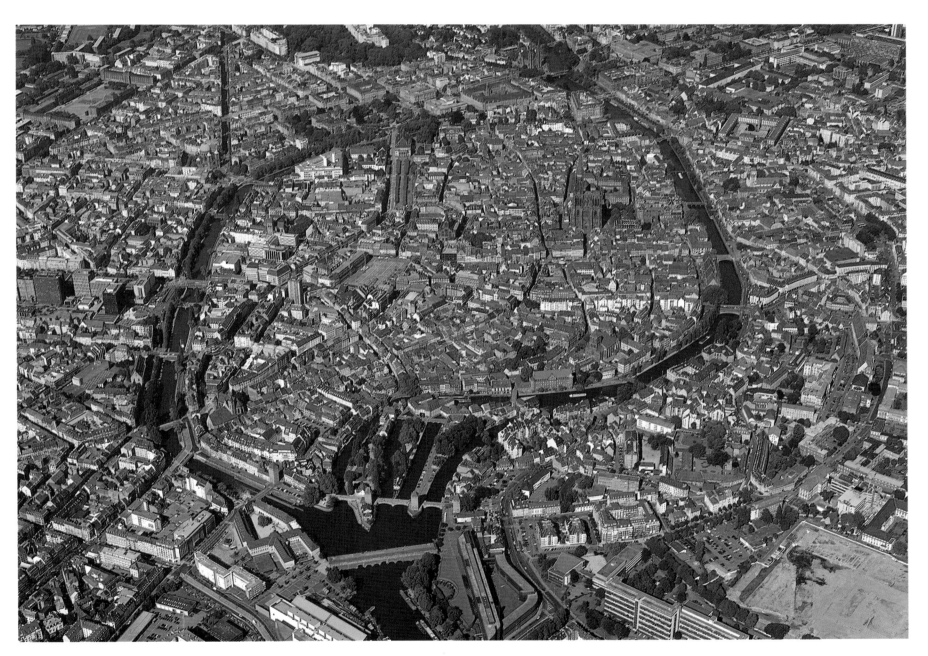

Aerial photo of Strasbourg seen from the west. The heart of the medieval city is encircled by the old stronghold canal to the north and the river Ill to the south. In the middle is Place Kléber.

The city

As the host city for the European Parliament, the Human Rights Tribunal and a number of other international institutions, Strasbourg has become a European capital, and this new position and obligation have been an important catalyst for the extensive urban renewal carried out since 1990. With 255,000 inhabitants and a regional population of 435,000, Strasbourg is not a large city by European standard. However, due to its location on the Rhine and as the main city in the province of Alsace, near the German border, the city has held an important position in European history and politics for centuries.

This is also one of the reasons for the selection of Strasbourg as the seat of important international institutions.

Strasbourg has a long history, first as a Roman border town and later as a vital cultural and commercial hub in a disputed border region. The centre of the city still has the charming character of the Middle Ages, with narrow, winding streets, priceless historical monuments and many well-preserved half-timbered houses.

The old city centre lies between the river Ill and the wide Fossé de Faux moat, and covers an area 1 x 1.5 km. The historic centre is ringed by newer urban quarters from various periods, which include the railway station with its large forecourt, Place de la Gare, a good 500 metres west of the city centre.

Along with the many politicians and bureaucrats from the large institutions, 50,000 students help colour daily life in the city. Downtown has a large share of residences, and was designated a World Heritage Site by UNESCO. The city is also a very popular tourist destination.

A combined strategy for public space and public transport

The drastic restructuring of public space and traffic started in about 1990. The traffic situation had grown steadily more chaotic year after year. At

Above: Place Kléber. Here in the middle of town, the new trams run quietly through the pedestrian areas.

Left: The main street, Rue de Franc-Bourgeois before and after the introduction of the new tram lane and the refurbishing of the street. View towards Place Kléber.

the time 240,000 cars drove into or through the city centre daily. In only a decade, traffic had increased by 20%. The old winding streets were unable to handle that kind of traffic pressure, air pollution had damaged the Cathedral and other valuable buildings, and all in all the heart of the city had become extremely unattractive due to growing traffic. A survey of travel habits from 1989 showed that 73% drove cars, 11% took the bus, while 15% bicycled or walked on their trips to and from the city. Attempts had been made for several years, but first under the leadership of Mayor Catherine Traumbert in 1989 was it possible to adopt plans for long-term urban renewal in which city life, bicyclists and public transport were given high priority, and car traffic in the centre reduced dramatically.

The plan was designed in three stages. The first stage was to establish a ring road, which was inaugurated in 1992. At the same time, the centre of the city was closed to most through traffic, the second stage in the plan. The third and most crucial step was the introduction of a brand new collective traffic system – a 12.6-kilometre tram line with elegant, comfortable carriages. The first tram line, Line A, was inaugurated in November 1994.

A linear public space policy in which trams pave the way

With the introduction of the new north-south tram line, a comprehensive, linear public space policy was well on its way. Pedestrians and bicyclists were to have much better conditions, the deteriorating spaces of the city were to be renovated and the new tram line to have first priority in city traffic. These objectives were combined into a strategy in which laying the tram tracks was the inspiration for rethinking all of the squares, streets and roads touched by the tram along its long route through town. Thus both suburban and inner-city spaces were renovated gradually as work on laying the new tram tracks progressed. In the city centre itself, several streets were completely closed to car traffic and reserved for Line A and pedestrians. At the same time, streets were renovated from facade to facade.

The new trams have an elegant, transparent design. Large, low windows provide a good view inside and out, making passengers part of the street scene at stops and while riding through town. An unusually low floor ensures good access for everyone.

Right: Platforms are directly on the level of the floor of the carriages at tram stops.

Far right: Outside the city centre trams have their own lanes. Traffic lights change automatically to green as trams approach.

In other streets, a modest stream of car traffic was allowed alongside pedestrians, bicyclists and the trams. In the suburbs, the tram tracks were laid in their own lanes, a guiding principle that also reduced the amount of room available for car traffic. Line A has a total of 22 carefully designed stops and ideal speed is calculated at 22 km/hour. On busy routes trams run every three minutes.

The strategy of allowing the tram lines to pave the way for urban improvement has had many interesting side effects. The most important squares in the city centre have been renovated, streets have been repaved and refurbished and greenery has been introduced. Further out on the periph-ery, this linear public space policy has often led to planting trees and establishing green areas. Landscape architect Alfred Peter has had the main responsibility for developing this visionary, green urban program.

"Le Tram" – and tram lines

A modern tram was selected as the new means of transportation in competition with bus systems and underground rail systems. Strasbourg's citizens were involved in the selection process, which clearly pointed to a modern tram that travelled along the street, rather than an unmanned underground Metro system, as in Lille, Lyon and soon in Copenhagen. Bus systems offered cheaper solutions, but were rejected by potential passengers as being uncomfortable. Popular preference was for trams at street level, with the exception of a short stretch where Line A tunnels beneath the railway station.

The carriages were specially designed for traffic at eye-height, with large, low windows that provide a good view from both inside and outside. Thus both when they wait at stops and while they are riding through the streets, passengers are part of the street scene. Each tram can carry 240 passengers and the unusually low floor of the carriages allows easy passage on and off for all categories of travellers. Both the exterior design of the carriages and their interiors are characterised by high design quality and provide a travel experience very much on the level of that in the newest trains.

All in all, Strasbourg has met a standard that is very rare for collective urban traffic.

The tram system in Strasbourg has become such a success in a very short period of time that it has exceeded all expectations. Only a few years after their introduction, the city's new trams carried 70,000 passengers every day, compared to the forecast of 50,000. Since 1990 the use of public transport has increased by 43%, and the number of trams serving the city centre has been doubled by introducing an extra line on part of the line A route.

Line B running east-west was inaugurated in November 2000, along 12.2 kilometres of track. Even more lines with a total track length of 35 km are on the drawing board.

Parallel with improvements in public transport, considerable efforts have been made to strengthen bicycle traffic by building bicycle paths and routes as well as supporting initiatives to allow people to take their bicycles with them on trains and trams. Initiatives like this have allowed Strasbourg to maintain its position as the leading bicycle city in France. Parking policy supports the city space objectives. One important link is three Park and Ride facilities that provide 1,700 parking spaces along tram Line A.

Drivers can park in these facilities for FF 15 per day, which includes free tram travel to and from town for themselves and all their passengers. Not surprisingly, these parking facilities have become very popular. Four more Park and Ride facilities are being built along Line B, and 1,000 parking spaces in the inner city are being abolished.

Place de la Gare has been converted into a pedestrian square with one large cohesive granite floor. Beneath the square are a tram stop and a shopping arcade, which enjoys daylight through a horizontal glass roof running along the railway station.

Public space in Strasbourg

Strasbourg has implemented a versatile policy that improved public space in both the centre of town and the periphery, reduced car traffic and reinforced energy-friendly means of transportation, pedestrian traffic in particular. The renovation program was carried out on the basis of a unified design policy in which the same materials, colours and furnishings are used throughout the city.

The most important public spaces along the tram route have been given very careful treatment, particularly Place Kléber, the main square, Place de l'Homme de Fer, the city's main public transport interchange area, and Place de la Gare, the expansive square in front of the railway station. The renovation of the first two squares is described later in this book. The large railway square, Place de la Gare, is a junction between the railway and Line A, which crosses beneath the station in a tunnel, with a stop underneath the square. The stop is connected to the station as well as an underground shopping arcade. A horizontal, transparent glass roof allows daylight into the underground area and also makes a distinctive presence in the large, very simple granite floor of the station square. Like everything else along the Strasbourg tram route, Place de la Gare has been renovated and simplified.

Public spaces from Strasbourg featured in the collection of projects:
Place Kléber: p.148
Place de l'Homme de Fer: p.152

Above: To see and be seen! The old part of the city has many good opportunities for recreational and social activities, such as here at the Cathedral square.

Below: The hectic activity of the main tram stop at Place de l'Homme de Fer stands in contrast to the relative quiet near the Cathedral.

Freiburg

Germany

Pioneers for a people-oriented city

Freiburg is a small European city with centuries of tradition. Starting in the 1960s, Freiburg gradually developed a green traffic policy that gave high priority to trams, bicycles and pedestrians. In parallel, the city worked to build and develop the city core as an attractive pedestrian area, maintaining the old street pattern in rebuilding the city after the destruction of the Second World War. The spaces of the inner city are connected architecturally by the reinterpretation of an old system of small streams running through the streets. The water element throughout the city makes Freiburg one of Europe's most attractive urban playgrounds.

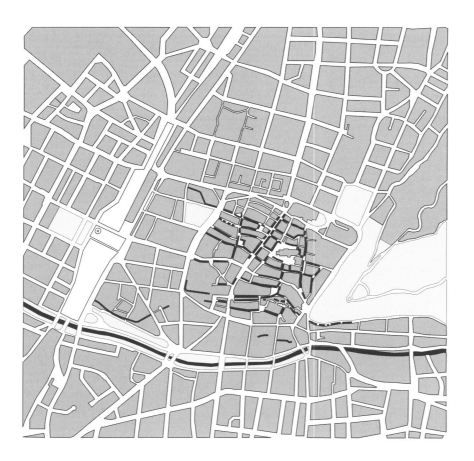

N

100 200 300 400 500 metres

1:20,000

Left: The city centre. Dark blue lines show the system of small streams – bäckle – that form a repeated architectural theme in the public spaces of Freiburg.

Aerial photo of Freiburg seen from the south. In the middle and to the right are the core of the city from the Middle Ages, the Cathedral and the wide main street. To the left is the railway station and the new bridge for bicycles, pedestrians and trams.

The city

With 200,000 inhabitants, Freiburg im Breisgau is by no means a large city. However, despite its relatively modest size, the city is characteristically European in terms of design, function and history. Freiburg is located in the Rhine Valley in the southwest corner of Germany, close to the borders of both France and Switzerland. The city is part of a string of towns built in the 1100s by the Dukes of Zähringen, as part of the consolidation of the League of German Princes in southwest Germany and Switzerland. Bern in Switzerland is another characteristic city in this group of fifteen. The Zähringer towns were built very exactly, according to a set of common planning guidelines. One common trait is the wide main street that also served as a market.

In the following centuries, Freiburg served as a fortification and border town under Austrian, French and German rule. The city maintained its medieval core, not spilling over into new areas until the 19th and 20th centuries.

During the Second World War, the city was subjected to heavy aerial bombardment in November 1944, and 80% of the historic city centre was totally destroyed. After the war, the inner city of Freiburg was rebuilt with great respect for its original character and history.

The extensive work on the traffic and public spaces of the city is rooted in this same tradition.

Today Freiburg is a lively city with a core strongly marked by a wide mix of functions. 7,000 people continue to reside in the city, while 12,000 students study at the university in its midst. Various institutions of higher learning are located near the city centre, and a total of 35,000 students attend classes in the middle of the city. As in the case of many other university towns of this size, Freiburg's status as a university town has had great influence on the vitality of the city as well as on traffic and urban policies.

The streets in the centre of town are restricted for use by pedestrians, bicyclists, and public transport. The small streams coursing through the streets help define the pedestrian area.

The city, traffic and public spaces

In contrast to many other cities destroyed by war, Freiburg chose to re-build on the basis of the historic network of streets and squares, maintaining original building lines and site dimensions with very few adjustments. One distinct city policy formulated by the head of planning, Joseph Schlippe, rejected the idea of widening streets to make room for growing car traffic, as was being done in many other rebuilt German cities. Instead car traffic was moved to a ring road around the city centre, while trams and bicycles continued to serve the city centre.

The first car-free streets and squares were established in 1968 around the Town Hall and Cathedral. In 1973 this development continued with the establishment of a large interconnected pedestrian area that comprised almost the entire core of the old city.

Freiburg became a pioneer in the work to rebuild German cities, with respect to developing an overall policy to reinforce pedestrianism, bicycles and public transport. The city started early, and particularly over the last 20 years has made extensive efforts to establish a green, pedestrian-friendly city with a balanced traffic policy.

A finely meshed network of bicycle paths and five tram lines serves the town. In 1990 daily bicycle traffic to and from the centre of the city comprised 43,800 bicycle trips. Ten years later in 1999 the number had risen to 71,400, an increase of 63%. Bicycles represent a total of 28% of commuter traffic, while public transport moves 26% and cars 46%. Cars have limited access to the city centre for running errands and making deliveries. 200-300 cars can park along the streets and squares of the city centre, while most parking spaces are located in car parks outside the city centre, often near tram lines. These parking facilities have room for 4,950 cars.

All five tram lines serve the city centre and the streets in the inner city. Outside the centre of the city, tram lines have their own lanes, with the traffic lights regulated electronically to avoid waits at intersections.

Above: The streams along the streets provide functional and visual separation between the pedestrian area and the tram tracks.

Below left: "Infomercials" on tram carriages are one means of communicating the city policy objective to conserve resources.

Below middle: Tram lines outside the city have their own lanes. Traffic lights are regulated electronically from the trams to ensure faster travel for public transport.

Below right: A bridge for pedestrians, bicyclists and trams crosses over the railway station. Stairs and elevators provide comfortable access. Left in the photo: bicycle parking in the new "mobility station".

The many streams turn the city centre into a wonderful playground. Never underestimate the creativity of children and anyone looking for a parking space.

The special tram lanes ensure faster public transport, a mandated prerequisite for state support.

A special bridge for trams, pedestrians and bicyclists that crosses the railway station and leads directly to the tracks has reinforced the popularity of these three forms of traffic. In 1999 a "mobility station" was built in direct connection to the railway and the bridge. The "mobility station" contains monitored bicycle parking so train commuters can park their bikes close to the train station. The building also contains bicycle repair shops, car-pool parking, tourist information and a cafe.

Pedestrian-friendly inner city

The streets and squares of the inner city are connected visually by two distinct elements found in almost all of the spaces of the city. One is a system of small streams while the other is decorated pavements laid with dark stones along the buildings of the city.

Freiburg is a river town, built on the banks of the river Dreisan running through the city just outside the centre. The whole city is located on a slight incline that falls 1.5% toward the west. Very early in the history of the city – mentioned for the first time in 1248 – river water was diverted into small streams that ran through the streets. The streams are 20-50 cm wide and 5-10 cm deep and in the past served as both water supply and waste-water runoff. The whole system of small streams has now been renovated. Streams that had been covered have been reopened, and today the small streams – called "bäckle"– make a lively and original contribution to the street scene. As a rule the streams are placed asymmetrically in the streets, defining and emphasising the linear courses and serving as a constant reminder of the city's status as a river town. The streams provide both sound and movement and in many streets also serve a useful function as marker and limitation between pedestrians and tram lines. Freiburg's streams are a lively temptation and challenge for the children of the city. In every street children can splash and wade, sail small paper boats and get delightfully wet. With its many small streams, Freiburg has one of Europe's most well functioning urban playgrounds.

It is city policy to lay natural stone in all pedestrian areas. Large surfaces are laid with granite blocks, while sidewalk bands of small, primarily dark local stone are used along the facades. These courses of specially selected small stones are an old German tradition, given a new interpretation and subsequent implementation that are very much characteristic of the Freiburg street scene. The sidewalk bands contain round symbols that tell what kind of shops and businesses can be found along the street. The symbols are designed according to a set of common guidelines, and the shops pay for the cost of having them laid.

The basis for the attractive city core in Freiburg is the careful rebuilding of the old, narrow and curving street network, combined with the consistent use of two venerable city traditions, the streams and bands of stone. All three elements derive from the city's history, but have been interpreted and adapted to the city as it is today.

Freiburg has worked to develop a green traffic policy on sustainable principles in combination with an attractive, pedestrian-friendly city core. Although good results have been reached on both accounts, the combination has also led to numerous conflicts and problems. There is heavy impact from the five tram lines that run back and forth across the city centre, leading to dense traffic on a number of the streets, particularly the hub at Bertold's Well.

The competition for space between pedestrians and the many tram lines is noticeable here. It is characteristic of public space policy in Freiburg to give traffic and movement in the city first priority. Trams, bicycles and pedestrians have good conditions overall, but there has been very little emphasis on creating good facilities for recreational urban activities. There is, at this point in time, too much going on and too little room for

sitting and lingering in the streets, and with the exception of Cathedral Square, the squares of the city have not really been developed as places to stop and stay a while.

However, the city has a lot of potential in this area, and a number of projects have been planned to develop it.

Above: Although conditions have been improved for bicyclists and pedestrians, less has been done to provide room for people who want a quiet place to stop and rest.

Left: One characteristic feature is the finely-crafted stone bands along the facades. Inlaid symbols tell the story of the types of shops and professions nearby.

Copenhagen

Denmark

A better city step by step

Copenhagen's old main street was pedestrianised in 1962, marking the start of what was to become extensive renovation. Over a period of four decades, many of the streets and squares in the inner city were gradually transformed into wholly or partially car-free space. This created good conditions for walking and urban recreation activities in the city centre. Systematic studies of the development of city life show a marked increase in activity in step with improvements. Cutting down on the traffic in the city centre along with gradually reducing parking options has helped limit car traffic in the inner city substantially. At the same time, a targeted policy to create better conditions for bicycle traffic has strengthened Copenhagen's position as a biking city.

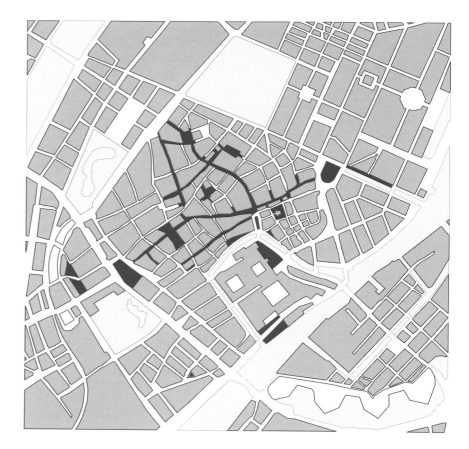

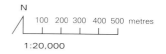

N

100 200 300 400 500 metres

1:20,000

Above: Map showing the medieval city core, plus part of the harbour and adjacent neighbourhoods. Dark lines indicate the extensive network of car-free or almost car-free streets and squares established gradually between 1962-2000.

Aerial photo of Copenhagen from the north. In the middle between the harbour and newer quarters, the core of the city from the Middle Ages. Right foreground: Amalienborg, Royal Palace Square.

53

The city

Copenhagen is Denmark's capital and greater Copenhagen has a population of 1.3 million inhabitants.

The city was founded around 1100 and grew gradually from a small fishing village protected by a castle to a lively trading port. The name Copenhagen means "merchants' harbour".

In terms of structure, Copenhagen is a typical European city, which grew within shifting fortifications surrounding its harbour, giving the city its characteristic shape. Large segments of the moats and ramparts of the 1600s and 1700s are still intact and serve as some of the city's parks.

Although major fires in the 18th century erased almost all traces of the buildings of the Middle Ages, the inner city, which comprises about 1 x 1 kilometres, has largely maintained its medieval street pattern. The buildings in the inner city derive primarily from the period after the great fires. They are four- to five-storey buildings with relatively short facades, which give the streets of the city an interesting and varied rhythm.

Although shifting periods left their mark on the buildings, large areas have maintained the simple neo-classic style that dominated the beginning of the 1800s.

The inner city continues to be Copenhagen's most important business area, with both fashionable shops and department stores, but it serves a wide variety of other functions as well.

Many of the buildings in inner Copenhagen still have shops on the ground floor, offices in the middle storeys and residences in the top storeys. A total of 6,800 people live in the inner city, which by European standards is a relatively high number of urban residents. The city core also contains many cultural institutions, large segments of the university and other institutions of higher learning with a total of 14,000 students. Thus given its scale and versatility, the city core has many of the basic elements needed to develop a good urban environment.

Public space policy – many small steps toward a better city

In the years up to 1962, all the streets and squares of the city centre were used intensively for car traffic and parking, under pressure from the rapidly growing fleet of private cars. In the years that followed, both traffic and parking, which had gradually come to dominate the inner city, were reduced or pushed back. A large number of streets and squares were converted to pedestrian areas, which today give the users of the city very attractive conditions for walking and all kinds of urban recreation activities. Pedestrianisation began with the city's main street, Strøget, which was converted in 1962 as an experiment. During the rebuilding of German cities after the Second World War, a number of pedestrian streets were established and it was these trade-oriented streets that served as an inspiration for Copenhagen. Despite the precedent, the conversion of the 1.1-kilometre Copenhagen main street into a pedestrian street was seen as a purely pioneering effort, which gave rise to much public debate before the street was converted. "Pedestrian streets will never work in Scandinavia"was one theory. "No cars means no customers and no customers means no business," said tradesmen. Other voices claimed "we are Danes, not Italians"or "there is no tradition for outdoor public life in Scandinavia,"which was true enough. However, the Danes had never before had the room and the opportunity to develop a public life in public spaces.

In no time at all, Strøget proved to be a huge success as a pedestrian street, in both popular and commercial terms. It did not take long for the tradesmen on Strøget, as well as in the other Danish towns that acquired pedestrian streets, to discover that the traffic-free environments were a valuable inducement to increased turnover.

More conversions of streets and squares followed in subsequent years. In 1968 the first north-south pedestrian street was established, followed by another in 1973. Gradually a cohesive network of pedestrian streets was

Left: Until 1980 Nyhavn along the waterfront was a car park for 78 cars. After renovation it has become the city's most popular walking street. On a summer day 1,000-1,500 people can be found sitting at cafes, on benches or the quay.

developed, offering today a truly effective system of transport for people on foot. It is easy to walk around in Copenhagen from one end of the city to the other, and today foot traffic represents about 80% of the movements in the inner city.

Already in 1962, parking on the squares along the new pedestrian street was reduced and recreational city activities began to develop. Over the next 30 years parking has been removed from a total of 18 squares, and all these new car-free spaces have been placed at the disposal of city life. When Strøget was pedestrianised in 1962, the city's pedestrian area comprised 15,800 square metres. 38 years later in the year 2000, the area of car-free streets and squares has grown to almost 100,000 square metres, or more than six times as many square metres reserved for public life.

The gradual expansion of the system of car-free and almost car-free spaces in the city has had three obvious advantages. City residents have had time to develop a completely new city culture, to discover and develop new opportunities. Correspondingly, car owners have had time to get accustomed to the idea that it has become more difficult to drive to and park in the city centre, but much easier to bicycle or use public transport. Thus people have had time to change their traffic habits and patterns. Finally it has become easier for the city's politicians to take the many small step-wise decisions on the basis of previously successful measures.

These many small decisions have led to an unusually attractive city centre, a relatively modest number of cars, and a profusion of public life quite extraordinary by Scandinavian standards.

All in all a development that must be attributed to a strategy of many small steps.

City space and traffic policy

In order to free space for the new city life, parking in the inner city has been reduced by 2-3% annually over many years. Motorists have gradu-

Above: Copenhagen's main street, Strøget, was pedestrianised in 1962. The 1.1km street crosses four squares including Amagertorv, shown here. This square was improved step by step like the other streets and squares in the city. In 1996 Amagertorv was repaved with a patterned granite floor designed by sculptor Bjørn Nørgaard.

Left: A parallel street, Strædet, was converted into a pedestrian priority street in 1989. Photos from 1988 and 1995.

ally grown accustomed to paying more to park or to leaving their cars at home, taking public transport, walking or bicycling in the increasingly more comprehensive network of bicycle paths.

The bicycle path network has been expanded year after year, and today the opportunities to bicycle in Copenhagen are so good relative to driving a car that many people prefer bicycling to work. Of the people who commuted to Copenhagen at the end of the 1990s, slightly more than a third bicycle, about a third drive cars and the last third use public transport to go from home to work.

Bicycling is once again a rather safe and uncomplicated mode of transport in Copenhagen, and it is not unusual to see the head of the Royal Theatre or a Minister of Parliament bicycling to work through the streets of the inner city.

One interesting new initiative to promote the use of bicycles in the city is free city bikes financed by sponsors and advertising. The city bike system covers the inner city and comprises about 2,000 bicycles that can be borrowed the same way one borrows a shopping cart in a supermarket by leaving a deposit in the lock. A small deposit is all it takes to borrow a bike from one of the 126 bicycle racks spread throughout the city centre, and you get your money back when you return the bicycle.

Over the past 25 years, bicycle traffic in Copenhagen has risen by 65%. Car traffic throughout the whole municipality has been held about constant from 1970 to 1996, even though the number of cars in the metropolitan area as a whole has risen dramatically in this same period. The unchanged traffic level within the city limits in more than a quarter of a century is extremely unusual by European standards.

 Not until 1996 did car traffic in Copenhagen begin to grow beyond the 1970 level.

Car traffic in the city centre has been reduced by limiting the opportunities to drive as well as by reducing the number of parking spaces. About 600 parking spaces have been eliminated in the centre of Copenhagen over the past decade, and today the city has about 3,000 parking spaces, two-thirds of them at kerbside in the streets. In fact, the city operates just fine with far fewer parking spaces in the city centre than in the other Scandinavian capitals. Stockholm has 8,000 parking spaces in the city centre and Oslo has 4,800.

Projects in the inner city and surrounding residential areas

The City Architect of Copenhagen has described the architectural concept underlying the design of the public spaces in the core of the city as "pearls on a string". The individual squares along the city's main streets have their own design and are connected by simple surfacing of the streets between them.

Most squares have been designed using traditional Copenhagen materials and simple traditional designs, leaving room, however, for more experimental ideas as well. One repeated feature is the traditional sidewalk of concrete slabs laid in bands separated and edged by chaussé stone. In pedestrian and pedestrian priority streets the classic sidewalks have been replaced by street floors, often divided into a middle zone of concrete slabs edged by bands of granite slabs and cobblestones.

Renovation of public space started with the inner city and the conversion of streets into pedestrian areas. In the next phase, the squares in the city centre were renovated and changed into places where urban recreation activities where given a high priority.

In more recent years, work has been ongoing to renovate the squares and streets in a number of the adjacent residential areas. Sankt Hans Torv, described on page 96, is an example of a renovated square in a densely populated residential area. The municipal planners are now working to bring similar improvements to the city's large traffic areas and terminals in other parts of the city.

Left: Bicycle traffic in Copenhagen has grown by 65% since 1980. Bicycles are an important link in the transport system and handle 33% of commuter traffic.

Far left: The latest addition to bicycle policy strategy: 2,000 city bikes that can be borrowed free of charge from the 126 bicycle racks located throughout the city centre.

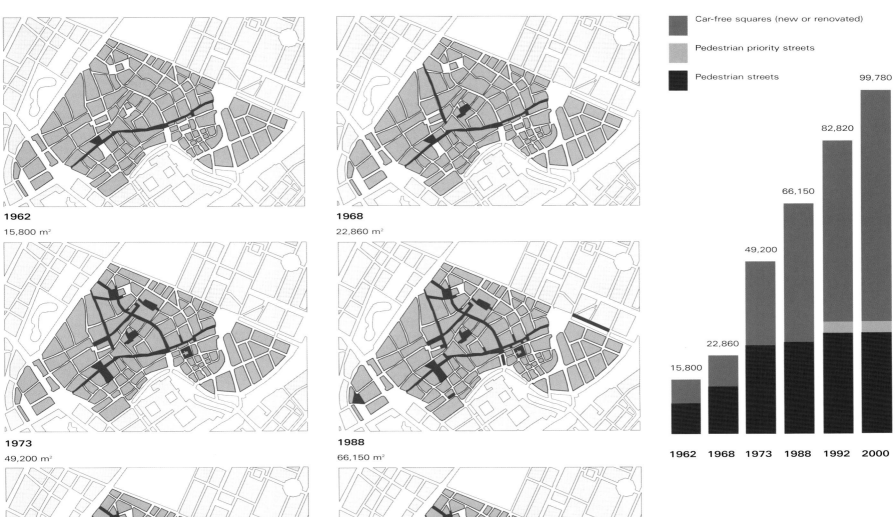

1962
15,800 m²

1968
22,860 m²

1973
49,200 m²

1988
66,150 m²

1992
82,820 m²

2000
99,780 m²

Car-free squares (new or renovated)

Pedestrian priority streets

Pedestrian streets

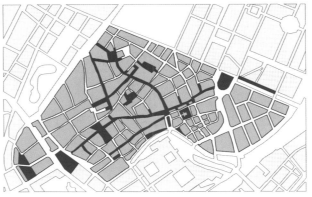

99,780

82,820

66,150

49,200

22,860

15,800

1962 1968 1973 1988 1992 2000

Above: The development of pedestrian areas in Copenhagen city centre from 1962 to 2000 in m². As shown by the bar graph, the conversion of streets into pedestrian streets was more or less finished by 1973. Subsequent efforts focused on reclaiming and improving the city squares. Of total car-free areas, streets represent 33% and squares 67%.

Left: 38 years of gradual expansion of the car-free network of streets and squares in the city centre.

57

From shopping streets to public forum

Almost all cities have systematic methods of gathering data and information about car traffic. However, it is extremely rare for cities to gather data on the development of pedestrian traffic and public life. Copenhagen occupies a special position in this area. Since 1968, researchers from the Centre for Public Space Research at the School of Architecture in Copenhagen have regularly recorded how public space is utilised and what changes and developments have occurred with respect to life in public spaces. A number of comprehensive studies of urban life throughout central Copenhagen in 1968, 1986 and 1995, supplemented with many smaller studies of individual locations, have made it possible to follow the development of urban life in step with the many improvements made since 1962. These findings have been documented in the book "Public Spaces - Public Life, Copenhagen 1996" published that same year.

The earliest studies from 1968 show that the then new pedestrian streets were popular as walking and shopping streets. However, when the first street musicians began performing for this new large public, utilising the good acoustics available once the cars were gone, they were shooed away by police. People were supposed to shop, not stop to listen to people play! Thus the pedestrian streets were at this point considered and largely used as shopping streets.

The study in 1986 shows the growth of a new and more active urban culture in which many more people participated in the exchange of talents, messages and alternative goods. The city's car-free space, which had vastly increased in the intervening years and now comprised more squares, had become "the country's largest public forum" according to a leading Copenhagen newspaper. It is important to note that this public forum requires no entrance fee or prior reservation, but is a place where anyone can turn up and participate, entertain others or be entertained. A very lively city centre has gradually developed.

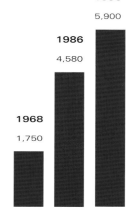

1995
5,900

1986
4,580

1968
1,750

The bar graph shows the extent of stationary activity – the number of people standing or seated – in the city centre in 1968, 1986 and 1995. The bars represent an average of four head-counts made from 11 a.m. to 4 p.m. on summer weekdays.

1968: Car-free area, 20,000 m²
Area per stationary activity: 12.4 m²
1986: Car-free area, 55,000 m²
Area per stationary activity: 14.2 m²
1995: Car-free area, 71,000 m²
Area per stationary activity: 13.9 m²

The latest of the city-wide surveys from 1995 shows that this development has continued, and now features heavy growth especially in the recreational activities of the city.

Pedestrian activities have been notably constant since the heavy growth immediately after the main streets were converted to walking streets in the 1960s and the beginning of the 1970s. The number of pedestrians in the streets has thus not risen in more recent years, among other reasons because street capacity is fully utilised for large periods of time. However, what has changed dramatically is the extent of non-walking activities. In the 27 years in which the development of public life has been followed, the number of people who engage in recreational activities on the streets and squares of the city centre on a summer day has increased by 3.5 times. In this connection it is interesting to note that the extent of the city's car-free area has also increased 3.5 times from the time of the study in 1968 to the corresponding study in 1995. Every time the city has expanded the pedestrian area by 14 square metres, another Copenhagener has turned up and set himself down to enjoy what the city has to offer.

A remarkable development of public life has emerged in step with improvements in the quality of public space. In only 27 years the summertime use of the streets and squares of the city has increased by 3.5 times.

One important factor in the large growth in stationary pedestrian activities has been the development of a cafe culture in the city. When the first pedestrian streets were established in the 1960s, outdoor cafes in Copenhagen were largely unknown. Since then, however, a cafe culture has grown gradually and today Copenhagen offers more than 5,000 outdoor cafe chairs, and on a good day, they are almost all taken. Thus, an entirely new city activity for Scandinavia – cafe culture – has developed over a relatively short period of time in step with changes in society and quality improvements in the inner city. A walking tour through central Copenhagen on a summer day shows a level and variety of activity and that was simply unthinkable 20 or 30 years ago. A new city culture has risen from the new city spaces, disproving the sceptics who said that Danes would never use public space.

The temperate Danish climate was given as yet another factor that would make it impossible or at least severely limit any attempts to develop public life in Denmark, and here too the development has been interesting. Outdoor serving starts early in the spring and continues later and later in the autumn. As Copenhageners have come to enjoy life in city spaces, the outdoor season has been extended and now stretches seven months from April to November. People are even talking about continuing all the way to Christmas.

The gradual transformation of the city centre from car culture to pedestrian culture has made possible a gradual development of city life and city culture. Copenhageners have grown accustomed to the new possibilities and have had the time and the opportunity to develop the versatile public life that is now characteristic of Copenhagen.

Public spaces from Copenhagen featured in the collection of projects:
Gammeltorv/Nytorv: p. 88
Axeltorv: p. 92
Sankt Hans Torv: p. 96

The Town Hall Square was renovated in connection with Copenhagen being the European Cultural Capital in 1996.

Right: Town Hall Square in 1995 before renovation.

Below: Renovation turned Town Hall Square into a large unified bowl-shaped space concluded by a pavilion building in dark glass.

Left: Copenhageners have become increasingly more enthusiastic about using their city. The outdoor season has been extended year by year and now starts on 1st April and doesn't end until 1st November. On cold days cafes provide cushions and blankets to help guests keep warm and enjoy outdoor life in the city as long as possible.

Portland

Oregon, USA

Pedestrian-oriented policy with detailed design guidelines

Inspired by grassroot movements and visionary politicians, Portland has demonstrated that it is possible to create a pedestrian-friendly city even in the country where the car is king. Trams that were discarded in the 1950s were reinstated in Portland in the 1980s, and today the city has a well-functioning public transport system of buses and several tram lines, which are free to passengers in the city centre. The design of the streets and squares and the relationship of buildings to public spaces follow a set of detailed design guidelines that emphasise top quality for pedestrians. Thus Portland has wide sidewalks with attractive surfacing, and numerous appealing parks and squares.

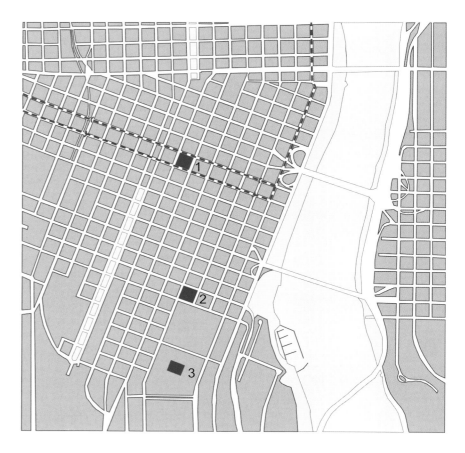

N

100 200 300 400 500 metres

1:20,000

Above: Map showing the city centre. The city follows a traditional North American grid pattern, but with a much finer network of blocks only 61x61 m. Dotted lines indicate the new tram lines. Pioneer Courthouse Square (1) is the main city square. Also shown: the location of two urban parks designed around 1970 by landscape architect Lawrence Hallprin: Auditorium Forecourt Fountain (2) and Lovejoy Plaza and Fountain (3).

Portland city centre seen from the south. At a distance the city looks like many other cities in North America. At street level, however, the city centre is distinctive for its careful design of public space and concern for pedestrians and public life.

The city

Portland is in the state of Oregon in the northwest corner of the USA. The city grew along the Willamette River, with the city centre on the west bank. Greater Portland is home to 1.5 million people, and has a typical North American grid pattern of streets and squares. However, its urban blocks are smaller than usual, which gives the city an atypical scale despite the tall buildings in the downtown area. The size of the urban blocks creates a different relationship between building mass and public space, as well as a different rhythm with large variation in the street scene. There is more space between buildings, and shorter distances from one street corner to the next, providing more opportunities for alternative routes even on short walks. Portland also has a more integrated urban character not dominated by the patchwork of parking spaces that disrupt the street scene in the centres of many other large North American cities.

Planning and public transport

Portland has a long tradition of good city planning, with citizen participation in the planning process and active grassroot movements. New plans for the city have gained momentum from the strong involvement of leading politicians in concert with an extensive number of public hearings. Portland's residents have always been very active in local issues, and in the 1970s the city moved the focus of its traffic planning. Emphasis shifted from unilateral car-traffic orientation to a more rounded view of the streets as a complex public space charged with meeting several needs. Pedestrians and public transport were accorded high priority. Portland's Arterial Streets Classification Policy made changes in the design of city streets. Traffic planners had previously considered the street network as primarily a transport system, with priority on increasing the road capacity for the growing stream of car traffic. However, after the 1970s, city spaces were classified according to their combined function, which led to varied demands for their design. In the downtown area efforts were made to provide broader sidewalks for pedestrians, with places to stop and rest, and easier access to safe street crossing. Parking and the amount of through traffic were regulated on the basis of overall use of the space. The road department's investments were also seen in a broader perspective. Investments were not meant to benefit traffic capacity and safety exclusively, but also to provide improvements to residential areas and other local interests. New plans for the city centre were drawn up with emphasis on public transport and improvements for pedestrians. In 1973 the state of Oregon adopted legislation to limit urban sprawl, so that new city functions could only be established within a fixed area designated within the Urban Growth Boundary. Zoning rural areas to protect agriculture and urban areas to limit urban growth gave Portland more concentrated building, which was an important prerequisite for the renovation and expansion of public transport. Portland had previously had an extensive tram network, which was dismantled in the1950s under the pressure of increasing car traffic. In the 1980s two new tram lines were established and the network has since been expanded several times. Already by the end of the 1980s, public transport carried almost half of the workforce to their downtown jobs. Bus and tram travel is free in the city centre, and the most important bus and tram lines cross at Pioneer Courthouse Square, which is the city's central public space and the hub for Portland's public transport options.

Civic pride and new city spaces

As early as 1970, Portland already had two unusual city spaces on the perimeter of the city centre. Lovejoy Plaza and Fountain from 1967 and the Auditorium Forecourt Fountain from 1970 were both designed by landscape architect Lawrence Hallprin, who created the powerful urban parks dominated by fountains and waterfalls emerging from stylised cliff

Far left: Trams have been reintroduced in Portland and lines are still being extended.

Left: The city is well supplied with specially designed tram stops.

formations. The establishment of the city's new main square, Pioneer Courthouse Square, is a fine example of significant urban changes that spring from grassroot activities. The project was not an easy one, as a car park several storeys high already dominated the space and had to be demolished. Then private funds had to be raised to pay for most of the conversion. An activist group of citizens who called themselves the Friends of Pioneer Courthouse Square raised more than 150 million US dollars from corporate and private sponsors to surface and furnish the square. This public sponsorship of the square is an interesting feature. For a minimal sum, people bought paving bricks with their name engraved. The stones were later laid alphabetically to pave the square. One reason for the great success of Pioneer Courthouse Square as one of the most well-functioning public spaces in the USA is summed up succinctly in "A Guide to Great American Public Places" by Gianni Longo: "One reason it works so well is that Portland residents, having fought and paid for it, own it."

Civic pride is palpable among Portland residents, even to casual visitors to the city. As one resident put it: "Portland is one of the few cities in America that gets better every year." Another resident mentioned that the traffic lights were timed for walking speed rather than driving speed, so pedestrians are riding a green wave.

Public space policy with detailed design guidelines

The key tenets of Portland's public space policy are formulated in its "Central City Plan Fundamental Design Guidelines 1990", which is a remarkable set of quality criteria for the design of the city's spaces. The city's intention is to strengthen the partnership between the public and private sectors to reinforce the identity of the city and to create a better place for its residents. Emphasis is on formulated guidelines to ensure a high quality in the urban environment for pedestrians.

Above: In addition to fine urban squares, Portland also has two distinctive city parks. Inspired by a natural waterfall and cliffs, they are designed by landscape architect Lawrence Hallprin.

Top: Auditorium Forecourt Fountain, 1970.

Right: Lovejoy Plaza and Fountain, 1967.

Portland wants to provide total solutions that surpass the usual standards of sectors working on their own, such as the public sector design of streets and the private sector design of individual buildings. The city council considers the guidelines to be a tool for generating good dialogue between the public and private sectors in order to ensure a better overall design of the city's physical surroundings. As the epilogue to the city's urban design guidelines states: "In summation, design guidelines are meant to encourage partnership between the public and private sectors to complement the urban setting in the spirit of design excellence."

The guidelines are divided into three main categories. First is Portland's identity, which describes the overall features of the city worthy of preservation or emphasis. Next is pedestrian priority, which sets out the criteria for the city's combined physical and visual environment. Last is project design, which primarily describes the quality requirements for buildings along the streets. Each category contains the background for regulation, the guidelines themselves and a detailed explanation of the quality requirements.

The first category, Portland's identity, gives eight guidelines for preserving the city's overall features. Portland's urban block structure is considered a distinctive part of the city's identity, which must be respected by any new building. Compared to other American cities, Portland's urban blocks are unusually small, only approximately 61 x 61 meters long.

In comparison, for example, the urban blocks in Seattle are about 244 meters long. The shortness of the urban blocks allows more light and air into the city centre, provides more route alternatives for pedestrians and spreads motorised traffic over a larger network of streets.

The guidelines emphasise the desire to preserve the special spacious character of Portland's streets and squares, the way public space caters to people and supports cafe life and other forms of outdoor urban life, and provides opportunities for urban recreation, places to sit and watch city

Top: Pioneer Courthouse Square is the city's main meeting place. The design supports many types of pedestrian activities and is also the hub for bus and tram lines.

Middle: Good benches under shady trees invite people to stop and stay awhile on the pavements of the city.

Right: Guidelines for buildings and squares emphasise the importance of street-level activity and opportunities for outdoor cafe service.

life go by. Portland wants to emphasise that the city is alive 24 hours a day and that public space should be seen as an urban stage for a diversity of human activities. Therefore planners want the buildings along the streets and squares to allow open contact between what is inside and what is outside and to contain a mixture of uses.

The second main category, priority for pedestrians, contains seven guidelines for the city's pedestrian environment. The main focus is to create quality in the overall environment for pedestrians. Here the guidelines span from general information on how to ensure the successful use of public spaces by creating environments that invite public use to guidelines with detailed requirements about providing good access to sunlight. Emphasis is placed on ensuring that city spaces are well defined, friendly and safe, and connected to other pedestrian areas. There is a detailed explanation of the division of sidewalks into zones covering various functions including a furnishing zone near the kerb, where sculptures, greenery and furniture are fitted, a centrally placed walking zone and a window-shopping zone along the facades of the buildings. Pedestrians are also protected against motorised traffic and ensured good opportunities to cross streets safely.

Portland wants to create barrier-free designs for the physically disabled that not only meet the requirements of building regulations, but provide solutions that are integrated into the overall environment.

The third and last group of guidelines concerns project design, and comprises 10 guidelines to ensure quality in building. Most of the requirements concern the relationship of buildings to public space, and emphasis is on well-conceived transitions between the insides of buildings and the public spaces outside. For example, buildings adjacent to parks and squares are required to fit in with outdoor activities and thus create active edge zones. The design of corner buildings should promote active crossing, preferably with entrances right at the corner. Skybridges and other forms of skywalks featured in many North American cities are to be avoided, but where allowed, they must be as transparent as possible to maintain visual continuity along the streets and the space underneath must ensure quality for pedestrians.

When Portland residents come to town, whether they pile out of their cars, descend from trams or get off their bikes, a set of urban design guidelines ensures that they can now enjoy a safe, accessible and interesting urban environment as pedestrians.

City spaces from Portland featured in the collection of projects:
Pioneer Courthouse Square: p. 232

Sidewalks are wide and divided into zones. Shown here nearest the kerb: zone for signs and furnishings, including sculptures, bus stops and benches. The middle is a pedestrian zone with room for window-shopping along the facades.

Curitiba

Brazil

Targeted efforts for sustainability, public transport and public space

Curitiba is a Brazilian city of more than a million inhabitants. Although the city grew at an unusually rapid pace, forward-looking planning harnessed growth while a versatile city policy gave the town and its citizens a better financial base and improved living conditions. Urban development has followed a five-finger plan with growth corridors built around central boulevards on which city buses, Curitiba's "metro on rubber wheels", have priority. Traffic, ecological, social, cultural and economic measures are elements in the city's overall policy that also comprises well-designed recreational areas and a very pedestrian-friendly city centre.

The results of the planning in Curitiba are unique in comparison with cities this size in other parts of the world with a similar economic development.

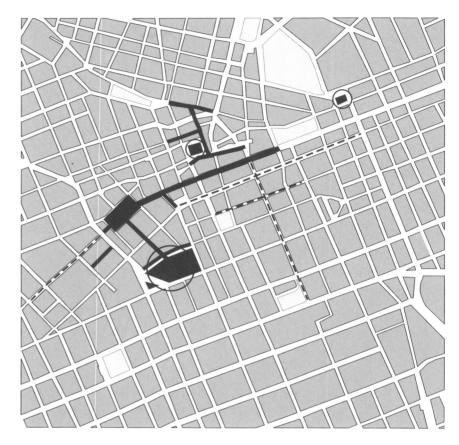

N
100 200 300 400 500 metres

1:20,000

Above: Map showing the heart of the city, with the most important pedestrian streets and squares indicated. Dotted lines show the pedestrian priority streets, while circles show the three bus terminals located in the centre.

66

Curitiba's five-finger city plan is reflected in the skyline. The buildings are high and dense in the city centre as well as along the public transport corridors, but much lower in the areas between the fingers. The precise management of the city's rapid growth is a vital prerequisite for implementing the other elements of the plan to achieve good urban quality.

The city

Today Curitiba has 1.5 million inhabitants. Located in southern Brazil, the city is the administrative centre for the state of Parana.

Portuguese colonists founded the city in 1693, and in the centuries that followed it was a backwater trading centre for the surrounding agricultural region. Immigrants from Germany, Italy, Poland and the Ukraine gradually became an important part of the local population, and in 1943 the city had a population of 120,000. The post-war migration to the cities of Brazil helped increase the population of Curitiba, which reached 470,000 people in 1965, an annual growth rate of 5.6%. In the 35 years from 1965 to the year 2000, the population of the city has tripled.

This rapid and expansive urban growth colours the way the city looks. It is still possible to recognise the traditional grid pattern from colonial times in the old quarters in the heart of the city. However, in Curitiba there is no such thing as a single network, but rather several street networks with various directions adapted to the landscape. The outlying districts of the town show the effects of various newer planning ideals. In addition to its functions as an administrative and cultural centre for the region, today the city supports active commerce and industry.

A recognisable trait in both the centre and the periphery is the dense building, with many high-rises that give the city its skyline. If we look more closely at the high-rise buildings, we can see some distinct principles at work. Unlike the majority of rapidly growing cities other places in the world, Curitiba has managed to channel and control its growth, and at the same time improve living conditions in a number of areas.

Controlled urban growth and visionary urban planning

The starting point has been a city plan from 1965, developed by Jorge Wilheim. The three main objectives of the plan were to lessen the traffic pressure on the city centre and preserve the historic core, to change

Top left: The large public transport boulevards are in the middle of the urban growth corridors. Here buses have their own lanes and specially designed bus stops.

Lower left: Three large bus terminals are located in the city centre making it easy to change buses and giving direct access to the network of pedestrian streets.

Immediate left: Each category of bus has its own colour.

urban growth from radial to linear along the transport corridors, and finally to restrict growth to existing areas of the city.

The plan was further developed in the years that followed, based upon a finger plan with five linear growth corridors stretching from the city centre. Each finger was built around a central boulevard with public transport, lined by tall dense buildings that diminishes in height the further one moves away from the transport corridor. Car traffic in the five corridors is carried along one-way streets, placed on both sides of the dense building mass, while only buses, bicycles and local traffic are allowed to use the central boulevards.

One important link in urban development was the establishment of an independent planning organ, the Institute for Research and Urban Planning (IPPUC), which faced major challenges and had mandates to match.

The planning efforts underway were further strengthened when architect Jamie Lerner, who had helped develop the plans, was elected mayor in 1972. In his three terms as mayor between 1972 and 1992, Jamie Lerner had major influence on the city's extensive and visionary planning. In 1992 Jamie Lerner was elected governor of the state of Parana, and was followed as mayor by Cassio Taniguchi, also a town planner.

Thorough planning, including effective public transport and many measures to improve both the urban environment and general living conditions, created a favourable investment climate.

A special industrial zone was built in 1973, and new zones have been added since. Today the city has considerably more new industries and workplaces than similar cities in this part of the world. In what might seem like a paradox, Renault, Chrysler, Volvo, BMW and Audi have all set up assembly plants in Curitiba, where public transport is given considerably higher priority than car traffic. Parallel with the physical changes in the city are extensive programs in social and cultural areas aimed at improving health, education, cultural opportunities and living conditions generally.

In almost every area that can be measured, Curitiba has reached a level considerably higher than the other cities in the country.

Curitiba's "metro on rubber wheels"

The effective organisation of public transport is a central element in Curitiba's planning. In a developing country with an economy much different from cities in Europe and North America, Curitiba selected buses as a means of public transport because they are flexible and considerably cheaper than trams and underground rapid transit. Instead the city developed its "metro on rubber wheels". It is a prerequisite for the efficiency of such system that people are able to get on and off the buses quickly and comfortably.

The bus system is organised around three guiding principles. Buses have their own lanes throughout the city, separate from the other traffic, which allows relatively fast transportation. Specially designed buses and stops ensure fast, comfortable loading and unloading of passengers. In addition, several bus terminals, some of them along bus routes and some at three major squares in the city centre, provide good opportunities for interchanges and good access from buses to the pedestrian areas in the city centre. A single ticket allows passengers to ride and get on and off throughout the whole bus system.

The transparent, pipe-formed bus stops, introduced in 1991, are an important link in efficiency. The floor of the stop is elevated level with the floor of the bus. Passengers step up at the stop, buy a ticket, and are ready when the bus comes. The ticket-sellers at the stops also operate the handicap elevators, and the presence of a bus employee at all of the city's 250 "pipe" stops naturally contributes to a friendly and secure atmosphere that is a well-known feature of Curitiba's collective traffic. The buses are specially developed for local traffic by Volvo in Curitiba. One special feature is the "gangways" that automatically lower to exactly

Immediate right: Buses and stops are specially designed. The floors of the bus stops are elevated and "gangways" on the buses ensure fast, safe loading and unloading for passengers.

Middle: At your service. The bus ramps are exactly the same height as the floors of the bus stops. This simple aid to getting on and off reduces bus stopping time markedly.

Far right: Bus stops have handicap elevators operated by ticket-sellers.

fit the openings at bus stops. From here passengers can go directly in or out. The whole operation including loading and unloading wheelchairs and prams is handled in a moment. All in all it has been possible to reduce waiting time for buses at stops by 80%, without causing passengers undue stress, and travel time has been reduced correspondingly. The buses are modern and well-maintained inside and out, and drivers have a good working environment due to the free bus lanes and not having to sell tickets.

The bus system is organised around four different types of lines. The categories are indicated by a colour code for the buses: direct buses are silver, express buses are red, cross-town buses are green and the rest of the lines are yellow. The newest express buses have three sections and can hold 270 passengers. Other buses have two sections and room for 160 passengers or are ordinary buses with 80 or 110 seats. The stops along the respective routes are designed so that the number of openings matches the number of doors for the type of bus. The largest stops have three doors. The whole system is planned and developed by mayor and architect Jamie Lerner. Curitiba's "metro on rubber wheels" is used daily by 1.7 million passengers, and handles 78% of commuter traffic. The average travel speed of the bus system is almost as good as that of metro systems, 30 km/hour.

An ecological capital

Curitiba wears its designation as the ecological capital of Brazil with pride, and in its work with ecology and sustainability surpasses most other cities in both developed and developing countries. The city's cheap and effective public transportation system is an important link in the planning. Other elements are sanitation, water purification, frequent collection of trash and sorting trash. An unusual program in this connection is 'green trading'; a scheme for the poorer households in the city, who are given fresh vegetables in exchange for carefully sorted trash. The ecological programs are largely tied to local areas and sections of town. Social and cultural institutions are correspondingly decentralised to strengthen the local areas. Interesting in this connection are seven municipal service centres set up in the seven large districts of the city. In the form of small service shops along a street, these "citizen streets" house a great variety of municipal and public services: healthcare, information, notary public, police, social centre, water, electricity, telephone, Internet, as well as meeting rooms and classrooms. The centres are placed along the transport corridors of the city and have been given a distinctive architectural expression. They have an easy-to-recognise, uniform colour program, despite any individual differences.

Lovely parks and friendly public spaces

The high population density of the city has prevented urban sprawl and been a prerequisite for the public transport. Population density has also made it necessary to provide good access to recreational options in the form of open areas, parks and public urban spaces.

Within the city limits, there are 26 woods and parks, and the newer parks are notable for their wealth of ideas and architectural treatment. There are parks with special reference to various groups of immigrants, while other parks have botanical gardens, opera or ecology as themes. Several of the new parks have been built in old quarries and dramatically exploit the differences in height as well as the naked cliff surfaces. Making parks out of the quarries has also prevented them from ending as rubbish tips, their fate in many other cities.

The city centre has developed as an unusually pedestrian-friendly area. From the squares with the many buses and stops, pedestrians walk into an extensive network of pedestrian streets and pedestrian priority streets. The latter in particular are impressive with their combination of wide

In recent years a large number of distinctive city parks have been established to provide good recreational opportunities in this densely populated city. Immediate right: Tanguá Park. Middle: Ópera de Arame.

Far right: Seven service centres offering many types of municipal services are located around town near the large public transport boulevards.

comfortable sidewalks, with one or two lanes for car access and parking. The pedestrian street system was started in the 1970s using the relatively low-key design of traditional urban models. The surfaces of decorative stone-laid patterns in black and white granite are inspired by public spaces in Portugal, and the unusually large number of benches draws a lot of people. Concern for the well being of its citizens is also expressed through the handicap policy that dictates orientation stripes in the pavement and lowered kerbsides at street corners. Another sign of the concern for both the city and people is the presence everywhere of municipal workers with a Curitiba logo on the backs of their orange uniforms, who are keeping the city unusually clean.

Compared to cities of its size in other parts of the world with correspondingly modest economies, the results in Curitiba are unique indeed.

A comprehensive network of pedestrian streets and pedestrian priority streets invites people to walk. The city floor is laid with decorative patterned stones inspired by Portuguese tradition. City employees in orange uniforms add hands-on concern for the well being of the city and its inhabitants.

Cordoba

Argentina

A unifying vision of public space architecture

In 1979-80, Miguel Angel Roca, the architect responsible for public works, formulated a unified strategy for an architectural, social and political city policy. The elements of the plan – the city centre as meeting place, the banks of the river as linear parks and nine local centres in the suburbs – characterise the structure and architecture of the city today. The policy for the city centre is based on an architectural concept for all the spaces of the city. Mirroring the monuments of the city with white marble bands on city pavements is one of several themes that provide visual unity between the many public spaces.

N

100 200 300 400 500 metres

1:20,000

Right: Map of Cordoba showing the city centre. Darker lines indicate the present network of pedestrian streets and squares that developed from architect Miguel Angel Roca's original plan for the unified architectural treatment of public space. The pedestrian network has been expanded several times since 1980.

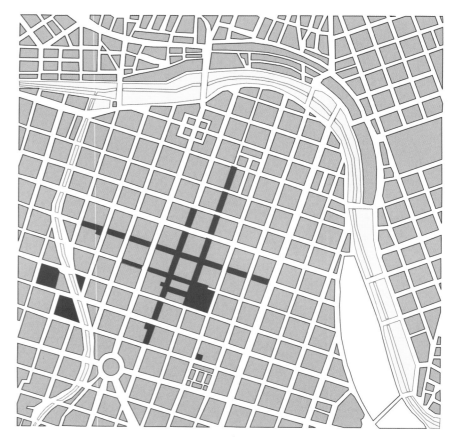

Aerial photo of Cordoba from the west. The winding Suguia River delimits the densely built city centre.

Aerial photo showing the character of the building at the periphery of the city centre. A small section of the denser city centre is visible in the lower right hand corner of the photograph. In the foreground are three of the city's distinctive public squares. Plaza Italia is shown near the lone skyscraper.

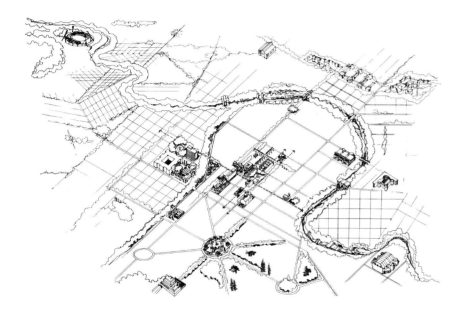

The city

Cordoba, which has 1.5 million inhabitants, is the second largest city in Argentina. The city is located 650 km northwest of Buenos Aires, on the border between the flat coastal plains and the mountains that rise towards the distant Andes. The city, which is the capital of Cordoba province, is a vital industrial and commercial hub with many administrative and cultural institutions. 200,000 students attend the city's universities. The city was founded by Spanish colonists in 1573 and laid out as a grid city in 110 x 110-metre blocks in keeping with colonial tradition. Particularly after the Second World War, the city grew considerably by adding amorphous suburban neighbourhoods, while the centre of the city kept its traditional system of urban blocks. Urban growth has put heavy pressure on the heart of the city with respect to functions and traffic. The city centre still has many valuable historical buildings as well as older two-, three- and four-storey buildings, and a large number of skyscrapers containing offices and dwellings. Today 75,000 people live in the 94 central blocks of the city, a remarkably high number of residents by international standards. In this same area 25,000 students attend classes, while 4,300 businesses and offices complete the picture of a very active, versatile and densely built city centre.

The city's transport system is based on buses and private cars and, apart from the pedestrian zone in the middle of the city, traffic density is extremely high everywhere.

An architectural and social city policy

In the middle of Cordoba, the visitor is struck at once by the many co-ordinated architectural expressions and statements that characterise the streets and squares of the city. These comprise the central and most visible part of an otherwise highly unified city strategy developed in the years around 1979-80, at the time architect Miguel Angel Roca was made

Upper left: Three-dimensional drawing of the elements of public space policy: treatment of the city's central spaces, linear parks along the riverbanks and the suburban centres.

Left: An ongoing theme in the public space policy is the decorative reflection of the facades of the city in the paved surfaces.

responsible for public works for the city. Within only 18 months of public office, he managed to formulate an unusually comprehensive architectural and political action program for the city. A number of projects were actually realised during this very short period of time, while others were carried out later.

The city strategy comprised three internally cohesive elements, all with the objective of encouraging social life and developing the identity of the city. The three-pronged plan comprises strengthening the entire city centre as a meeting place, developing the banks along the Suguia River as linear parks and, finally, bolstering the new neighbourhoods by building nine suburban centres with decentralised municipal service functions. The underlying idea was the vision of the metropolitan area as a collection of equal city neighbourhoods grouped around a central meeting place that would further strengthen the feeling of identity and sense of community.

The city centre as meeting place

The plan for the city centre as a meeting place is interesting given the efforts to formulate a unifying architectural vision for the public spaces of the city. The city's most important streets, squares and individual parks are unified in a public project in which common design principles, materials and details are meant to ensure the architectural identity of the city as a whole. The way in which the public space is depicted in Miguel Angel Roca's poetic drawings formulates and clarifies his architectural thinking. Although the streets and squares treated are not necessarily connected to each other physically, the public space is seen and depicted as a connected system in which the individual spaces each contribute their part to the total picture.

Miguel Angel Roca saw it as his job to design the space with a good framework for city life, while ensuring that the design also helps define

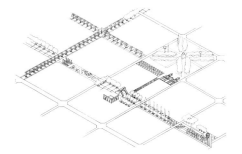

Left: The city's network of pedestrian streets and squares is envisioned and treated architecturally as one spatial entity.

Right: The facades of the cathedral and prefecture are outlined in white marble bands on the grey granite floor of Plaza San Martin.

and clarify the history and monuments of the city. His answer to this double objective was to mirror the city's most important monuments in the new stone floors of the pedestrian zone. The motif of the mirrored monuments executed in white marble on the grey granite surfaces is repeated several times in the city centre, adding an interesting extra dimension to the squares and streets. Together the floors and walls of the city create a new composition and the outlines in the floor of the city are a special, identifying feature of Cordoba.

Right: Parliamentary seats outlined on the street surface outside the Parliament building, a very literal interpretation of the expression: The Parliament of the street.

Below: Symbolic columns serve as gate and entrance to one of the streets. Outlines of the portico of the courthouse are embedded in the surface of the street.

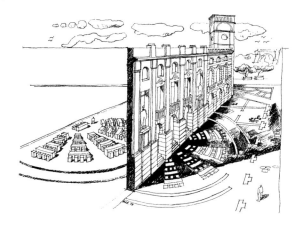

The streets and squares of the city

Although the mirror images can be seen as the most distinctive common trademark, it is characteristic for the treatment of the streets and squares of the city that sequences of space with various characters and tools are used. The character of the space in the central pedestrian street changes from section to section. The first has diagonal reflections of the facade of the university, marking the shadow of the building on the day and time the university was inaugurated. In the next section the objective was a strict, quiet street expression with two rows of poplar trees. Other street sections are without trees or repeat the motif from the previous sections of the street, ending in front of the government building for the province. Here the story of the parliament is told by outlining the chamber and seats on the floor of the street. People can indicate their political dissatisfaction by stamping on the white marble surfaces, a very direct interpretation of the Parliament of the street. On the same street the loggia of the Ministry of Finance is the motif for the pattern of the paving, and the street ends with two rows of one-storey concrete columns that serve as a gate to the area.

A distinctive furnishing element appears in the more commercial section of the pedestrian zone, a pergola of steel supporting a green roof for the 11-metre-wide streets. The roof of green plants provides shadow for pedestrians, reduces the noise from nearby traffic streets and forms an intimate ground-level space along the shops. The pergola system along the narrow streets is a relatively dominant element, but it also hides the many obtrusive signs above the shops. The pedestrian zone in Cordoba has been expanded several times since 1979-80, and although one can still detect the inspiration from Miguel Angel Roca, the newer pedestrian streets have less power and originality than the models on which they were based. Another important link in the public space policy of Miguel Angel Roca is the main squares, which just like the most important streets,

were renovated in the years around 1980. The central square, Plaza San Martin, formerly used as a car park, has a simple design with a large central park. The white marble bands that represent the outlines of the city's cathedral and prefecture comprise the primary decoration in the square. The intimate Plaza Malvinas has a reflecting pool shaped like a map of Argentina as a motif, while the dramatic Plaza Italia with its three fountains refers to the three fountains of Piazza Navona in Rome, as well as to the Po, Arno and Tiber Rivers and "the waters of Cordoba".

Few cities if any can match the comprehensive public space strategy of Cordoba, carried out within the framework of one distinctive architectural vision.

Above: Plaza Italia from 1980 with reference to the rivers of Italy and "the waters of Cordoba".

Left: The pedestrian sections form spatial sequences with various treatments within the framework of a unifying vision. The most important shopping streets have a shady roof of plants supported on steel elements.

Melbourne

Victoria, Australia

Unified policy for quality and vitality in city streets

With 3.3 million inhabitants, Melbourne is Australia's second largest city. Its history, street pattern and mix of high and low buildings in the city centre are reminiscent of many other large cities. However, where other cities have surrendered their streets to the automobile and developed indoor shopping malls, Melbourne decided to keep its streets as the city's most important public spaces. The city undertook extensive renovation of pavements and street furniture, reinforced its status as a green city and developed a policy for active facades along the sidewalks. Thus Melbourne has ensured that its streets invite people to walk.

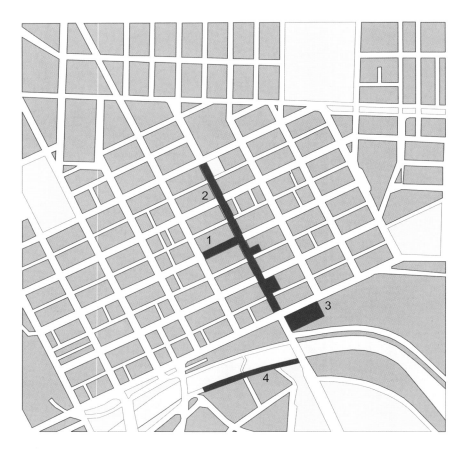

N

100 200 300 400 500 metres

1:20,000

Above: Map showing the centre of the city between the Yarra River and surrounding quarters. The street network is laid out in 200 x 200 meter blocks and contained no squares originally. Shown are the city's two pedestrian and tram streets Bourke Street (1) and Swanston Street (2), as well as the city's new square Federation Square (3) and the privately-owned South-bank area (4).

City of Melbourne from the south. The city centre lies between the Yarra River and the surrounding inner suburbs. Skyscrapers are primarily located along Collins Street, parallel to the river, while the main street, Swanston Street, runs through the city centre, at a right angle to the river, surrounded by lower buildings.

The city

Melbourne is the capital of the state of Victoria in the southeast corner of Australia. The metropolitan area has 3.3 million inhabitants spread out over a large number of suburbs. Thus the city of Melbourne has many institutions and offices but only about 45,000 residents.

The city is located along the Yarra River, a few kilometres from where the river meets the sea. The city was founded in 1835 at the point where it was no longer possible to navigate the river, and served as a trading post for the extensive agricultural regions in Victoria.

Today the city is a lively metropolis that supports trade, industry and many public functions. Housing is overwhelmingly single-family dwellings, and the city is spread over an unusually large area.

Unlike the expansive residential areas, the city centre is rather compact. The heart of the city with its dense tall buildings has a combined area of about two square kilometres.

The street network was designed according to the traditional block pattern favoured by the English colonists. In Melbourne the blocks are 200 x 200 metres, corresponding to ten surveyor's chains for each length. The streets were designed in widths of 1.5 chains and are thus a good 30 metres wide. These large blocks are intersected by a secondary system of streets running east-west, with smaller back lanes. A third street network, characteristic for Melbourne, is made up of the many internal covered arcades that cut through the blocks of the city in a north-south direction. The many small back lanes and covered arcades provide rhythm and variation to the otherwise rather rigid street pattern. Another characteris-tic feature of Melbourne is the absence of squares. Green areas and small parks are often found as forecourts to churches and monumental build-ings, but proper squares or marketplaces as they are known in older cities are not part of the pattern in Melbourne. Instead the city was provided with a number of large parks.

The city, cars and public transport

The expansive single-family residential areas outside the dense centre of the city and the large concentration of workplaces in its heart mean heavy car traffic to and from the centre of the city. An underground subway ring plus an extensive tram network help lessen traffic pressure to some extent. Melbourne has a long unbroken tradition of trams starting in 1869 and still running today. In about the year 1900, Melbourne had the third largest network of horse-drawn trams in the world, surpassed only by Paris and London.

There were no major changes for many years after the tram lines were electrified in the 1920s, but starting in 1980 the line network has once again been expanded and new tracks are being laid, particularly in the harbour area. Plying the city streets today are a colourful mixture of old trams and various newer models. The old green 'Melbourne trams' are a characteristic feature of the street scene, and specially decorated restaurant trams and art trams help underscore Melbourne's status as a tram city with more than a century of tradition.

A pedestrian-friendly public space policy

The trams are a special feature of Melbourne, helping to tie the history of the city to the conditions of today, and they play a natural part in Melbourne's public space policy. Whereas the majority of large cities in Canada, USA and Australia have been allowed to develop relatively freely on the conditions of motorists and market forces, Melbourne has made a major effort to maintain and develop several of the city's traditional qualities, including strengthening public life and pedestrian traffic in the streets of the city.

The public space policy was developed in the years after 1985 in connection with a change in the city's political leadership. A new Urban Design Branch with a large sphere of responsibility with regard to the city's

The public space policy is rooted in the long tram tradition of Melbourne.

Left: Swanston Street Walk, the city's main pedestrian and tram street.

Far left: New and old trams are part of the street scene. Shown here, a restaurant tram and an art tram.

public projects and public space was established, and a new policy was formulated under the leadership of urban design architect Rob Adam. Four sectors were designated as important qualities in Melbourne: the river and parks, the characteristic older urban quarters, the traditional street network and the tram system. Further development of these urban qualities became main themes in the new public space policy, and strengthening the city's streets and life in city spaces became a central and unifying link in the planning. Whereas streets in many other cities were more or less abandoned in favour of indoor pedestrian systems and malls, Melbourne decided to stimulate pedestrian traffic and vitality in the streets of the city, to invite people to get out of their cars and walk. This invitation is communicated in many ways. Melbourne has always been a green city, but it has become even greener with the planting of many new street trees. The city's main sidewalks have become broader with a distinguished new surface, bluestone, a local basalt stone that is the city's traditional building material. Many buildings are constructed of this stone and the city's major streets were originally laid with bluestone. This motif of bluestone surfaces has been revived and many kilometres of the city's pavements have now been renovated with the characteristic surfaces of large bluestone blocks.

The width of the pavements varies from three to eight metres, depending on the type of street, and renovation has largely been paid for by the city. In some cases building contractors have paid for the renovation under a bonus system that matches support for city quality by permission to increase the floor space in new constructions.

In the beginning of the 1980s, a number of large malls were established in the centre of the city. Their closed facades and pedestrian bridges that minimised street life and blocked the view served as glaring bad examples. Since then the city has formulated an active policy that addresses these areas. Indoor connections that cross streets are not allowed, and active, transparent ground floor facades facing city streets are a requirement. The renovation of the lighting in the city's major streets is another element in the unified city space policy.

The streets and squares of the city

Emphasising and improving the quality of the streets is a logical consequence of the street pattern in Melbourne. In the absence of squares, the city streets have always been important public spaces. Psychologically, the pattern of the all street city signals walk, walk, walk. The natural breaks and sites for stationary activities that city squares can offer do not exist in the traditional street network of Melbourne.

Given its urban pattern, Melbourne has developed some of its streets as pedestrian and stopover streets. In 1974 the city's first pedestrian mall was inaugurated in the central part of Bourke Street, a combination walking and tram street. In 1992 the city's main street Swanston Street was closed to private car traffic and renamed Swanston Street Walk. Now the street is a pedestrian and tram street with wide refurbished sidewalks. Squares and tram-free stationary activity areas are also in high demand as city spaces in the pedestrian-friendly city of Melbourne. In the 1970s a large Civic Square was established in front of the Town Hall on Swanston Street. However, due to an unfortunate function-oriented design with many small specialised spaces, the square was not successful. A redesign of City Square, slated for completion in the year 2000, and the ambitious new Federation Square are currently underway at a site near Flinders Street Station.

South of the river, on the sunlit bank, several privately owned squares have been established in connection with the Southbank Centre, a commercial and entertainment complex. In the absence of good squares in the city itself, these spaces have gained importance as recreational areas for public life, despite their private character and security surveillance.

Far left: In 1978 the central part of Bourke Street was converted into the Bourke Street Mall, a 200-metre-long pedestrian and tram street paved with red brick.

Left: Melbourne was founded as a city of streets without any squares. The private, commercial Southbank Centre, with its sunlit open spaces facing north, has become very popular in the absence of true public squares. Both buildings and paving were executed in the local bluestone.

City furnishings

The architectural theme for street renovation in Melbourne has been to emphasise the street motif. The linear character of the spaces is underlined by rows of trees and street lamps, and the regular wide sidewalk in particular communicates the message: this is a city street.

The Urban Design Office drew up a new program of street furniture for the new public spaces with their new bluestone pavements. The program includes a wide assortment of public space furnishings with perforated steel plates as the unifying material. A dark green colour that harmonises well with the colour of the pavement was chosen for the new benches, tables, screens, planters and litter bins.

The new city furnishings have been introduced throughout the city wherever new pavements have been laid. At the same time, older public furnishings as well as the jumble of private furnishings have been removed. Private cafe chairs in plastic and so on are not accepted on the serene new pavements. Instead outdoor serving establishments are required to use the city's official furnishings – green tables, chairs and planters – that can either be leased or purchased from the municipality. Because most Melbourne streets have trams and many of them car traffic as well, a transparent screen to protect guests from wind and noise was designed to stand between streets and outdoor serving areas.

The simple blue-grey pavement together with the uniform white umbrellas, glass screens and green furnishing are valuable elements that provide a sense of tranquillity and cohesion in the streetscape, which is highly mixed visually.

Public spaces from Melbourne featured in the collection of projects:
Swanston Street Walk: p. 250

Traditional bluestone paving was reintroduced as part of public space policy from 1985. The natural stone paving and furnishings in green-painted steel provide a dignified atmosphere in a heterogeneous cityscape.

Right: Sunday morning on Swanston Street Walk.

Below: A carefully designed program of city furnishings sets the scene. Cafe chairs and tables are purchased or leased from the Town Hall and planters, litter bins and other furnishing elements are executed in uniform materials and colours. A special screen of hardened glass was designed to separate outdoor serving areas from the streets.

northern europe
central europe
southern europe
canada
usa
saudi arabia
japan
australia

39 streets and squares

39 streets and squares: Introduction

This chapter contains 39 examples of public spaces – 36 squares and three streets. Together they give a good impression of the breadth of ideas and design expressions that characterise public space architecture in the years up to the new millennium 2000.

The examples are primarily central public outdoor areas, with a few courtyards of private office buildings or genuine monumental squares. The inhabitants of the given city or neighbourhood use most of these public spaces every day. In addition, most of the spaces give high priority to pedestrians and urban recreation activities.

These particular spaces were selected in order to show various urban situations, various types of public spaces and differences in architectural expression.

The examples fall into two main groups: existing public spaces subjected to extensive renovation and completely new spaces.

For the group of renovated city spaces, a characteristic feature is that the streets and squares often have a clear form defined by surrounding buildings. Here renovation consists primarily of an architectural reworking of the furnishings of the space, with emphasis on surfaces, lighting and inventory.

Projects span solutions with very subtle floors and simple inventory to expressive solutions with more experimental installations. In most cases renovation also includes a rerouting of traffic with priority given to pedestrians and urban recreation. In many cases this is combined with the establishment of parking under the street or square.

The group of new public spaces can again be subdivided into two characteristic groups. One includes squares created primarily by tearing down existing buildings, or by taking advantage of a change in the use of open space in the city structure. These areas often have diffuse or undefined spatial limits. A number of these projects stress the creation of spa-

tial clarity through a precise working of surfaces and the installation of dramatic spatial elements. Barcelona, for example, has a considerable number of squares and parks of this type.

Another group consists of squares in which both the space and the surrounding buildings were created in one unified architectural coup. The sequence of new public spaces in Montpellier, Broadgate Arena in London, the new public spaces in Riyadh, Saudi Arabia and Tsukuba Centre Square outside Tokyo are very different examples within this group of city spaces executed in connection with building large new complexes.

With respect to the main character of the spaces, the examples span squares dominated by hard floors and inventory in stone and steel, to spaces in which trees and other greenery are the main elements. Some of these areas are divided into several characters: the combination of a stone floor with a green space, for example, forming a composite character.

Ongoing experiments with lighting in public spaces are on the increase. Architects are playing with relatively dramatic differences in light intensity from subtle to bold, or with lighting that can vary the atmosphere and character of the space during the evening or create special lighting effects for special events.

Together the squares and streets selected paint a versatile picture of the wealth of ideas and creativity that mark the public space architecture of the period.

Each of the examples selected is shown in a plan in the scale of 1:2,000, as well as in two maps in the scale of 1:5,000, showing the building context and describing the area in which the project is featured. The location of the space in the city structure is indicated in a simplified map of the city on a scale that varies with the size of the city.

The location, type, history and main architectural feature of each project are described in key words.

Types of spaces

Main city square
The central square in a city, town or quarter, (Example: Place Kléber, Strasbourg, page 148.)

Recreational square
Public space with the primary function of meeting place or recreational activity. Lively squares as well as spaces with a more passive recreational character come under this category. (Example: Sankt Hans Torv, Copenhagen, page 96.)

Promenade
While this type of public space may provide furniture for stationary activities, it is the momentum or direction that is characteristic. (Example: Champs Elysées, Paris, page 140.)

Traffic square
The main function of this type of public space is to facilitate the circulation of traffic as well as the interchange between different modes of transport. The selected squares emphasise concern for public transport passengers. (Example: Luisenplatz, Darmstadt, Germany, page 30.)

Monumental square
This type of public space provides a pause in the city fabric and often has symbolic importance. The forecourts of monumental buildings also fall under this category. (Example: Squares in Qasr-Al-Hokm, Riyadh, page 240.)

Architectural features

Surface treatment
Squares and streets whose renovation largely involves surface treatment, with furniture and inventory as subordinate elements. (Example: Rathausplatz, St. Pölten, page 134.)

Surface and elements
Squares whose large spacious objects furnish the floor and influence the spatial composition decisively. (Example: Placa del Països Catalans, Barcelona, page 178.)

Composite character
Public spaces whose varied main elements divide surfaces into areas of distinctly different character, such as a combination of stone floors, water features and green areas. (Example: Placa del General Moragues, Barcelona, page 190.)

Combined square and building design
Squares in which both the space and the surrounding buildings were designed as one unified architectural composition. (Example: Tsukuba Centre Square, Tsukuba, page 246.)

The 39 projects are presented in regional order starting in Europe from north to south, followed by examples from North America, Asia and Australia.

The index on page 258 presents the public spaces described by location, type, history and architectural features.

Gammeltorv/Nytorv

Copenhagen, Denmark. 1991-92
Architect: Stadsarkitektens Direktorat, with architects
Sanne Maj Andersen and Leif Dupont Laursen

Location: City centre
Type: Central city square
History: Renovated public space
Architectural feature: Surface treatment

Gammeltorv/Nytorv is an example of the quiet renovation of an urban space in which buildings play the leading role and surfaces provide unity. The history of the square is told in the details of the pavement.

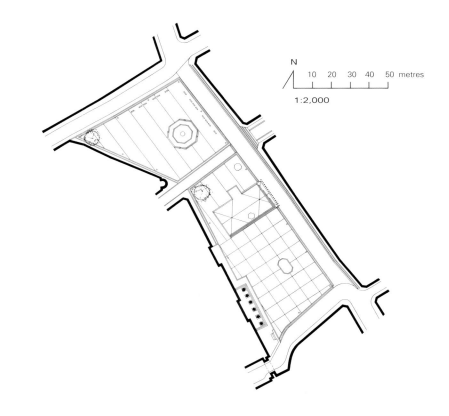

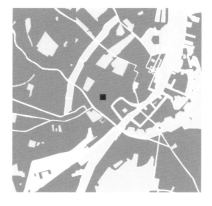

Copenhagen
1:100,000

Gammeltorv/Nytorv
1:5,000

Pedestrian zone: 7,300 m²
1:5,000

Right: Before 1962 the square was totally dominated by parked cars.

Below: Gammeltorv/Nytorv after renovation. Peace has been restored to public space and pedestrians have priority.

The city was founded in 1167 and today the city centre still has the winding street pattern of the Middle Ages lying within the boundaries of the historic fortifications with their partially preserved ramparts and moats. Gammeltorv and Nytorv are situated in the historic centre and present an open, slightly sloping square.

Gammeltorv is Copenhagen's oldest square, and served as the town hall square from about the year 1479, when the city's third town hall was built at its southern end. The square was expanded to include Nytorv after the building behind the town hall was torn down in 1606. The Cari-

tas fountain at Gammeltorv dates from 1608 and was once a festive contribution to the city water supply. The town hall burned down several times and after the great fire of 1795, the building was torn down completely, giving the space the form we know today, in which both Gammeltorv (old square) and Nytorv (new square) are united into one large, connected urban space.

Most of the buildings surrounding the square are in neo-classic style, which gives the square a relatively homogeneous and quiet character. A new town hall and courthouse were built on the west side of Nytorv after 1805. Gammeltorv/Nytorv lost its prominence as the city's main square in 1905, when the city council moved to the present town hall on Town Hall Square.

With the increase of car traffic after the Second World War, Gammeltorv/Nytorv was used for parking. However, in 1962 the space near the fountain at the old end of the square was incorporated into part of the pedestrian area when the city's main artery, Strøget, was pedestrianised. After renovations in 1974 and 1991, the new end was made car free step by step and today the entire square is one cohesive pedestrian area with a granite floor from wall to wall, emphasising its unity. A couple of bus lines continue to run along the eastern side of the square, while car traffic is restricted to the north and south sides.

The starting point for the redesign of the squares was to create a quiet background for the buildings, so that the space would stand out clearly. The chaussé stone floor unites the space across the terrain that drops about four metres from north to south. The history of the site is told in the details of the stone floor. The site of the former town halls that originally separated the old and new squares is marked as a rectangular horizontal plane creating a few steps in the sloping terrain. The outline of the most recent town hall is shown in the floor, which also contains a stone with information about the building and an illustration of its form.

Above: The Caritas fountain at Gammeltorv is a popular place for urban recreation.

Right: Chaussé stone granite paving unifies the floor of the square. The location of former town halls is marked on the surface. Information about the buildings and their history is included.

The new square contains the outline of the old scaffold indicated by a little plinth raised to seat height.

Over time both squares have been used for many purposes, from the jousting tournaments of mounted knights to public executions and bustling markets. Today Gammeltorv/Nytorv is one of the most popular of the city's squares for urban recreation, a place where people can sit and watch the ever-changing crowd of people from far and near who cross the double square at Strøget, the main pedestrian street. The square is host to a continuous stream of activities throughout the year, both ordinary and festive. Tents and podiums are set up for special arrangements. Jazz is played here at the annual jazz festival, symphony orchestras give classical concerts, and colourfully dressed folk dancers step to traditional music. In the summer the square is filled with outdoor cafes and Gammeltorv serves as one of Copenhagen's informal meeting places around the Caritas fountain.

Above: Hundreds of devotional candles are lit on the floor of the square in a moving memorial to AIDS victims.

Right: Relaxed morning mood. Shown in the foreground, the traditional Copenhagen benches found throughout the city.

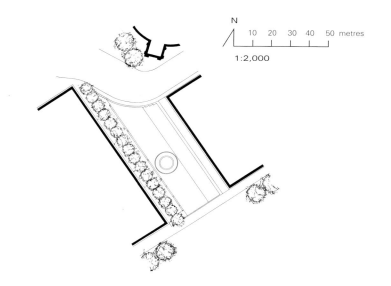

Axeltorv

Copenhagen, Denmark. 1991
Architect: Mogens Breyen
Artist: Mogens Møller

Location: City centre
Type: Recreational square
History: Renovated public space
Architectural feature: Surface treatment

Axeltorv is part of a newly established pedestrian axis that connects Tivoli Gardens with several other recreational options northwest of Copenhagen's famous amusement park. The square is based on very few but precisely articulated materials and furnishing elements, with emphasis on artistic decoration using the sun and planets as its theme. Although the square is an open public space, the owners of the surrounding buildings paid for renovation.

Copenhagen
1:100,000

Axeltorv
1:5,000

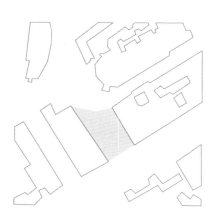

Square/Pedestrian zone: 3,600 m²
1:5,000

Above: Axeltorv during renovation

Axeltorv seen from northwest. Left is Scala Centre, with the main entrance to Tivoli in the background. The surface of the floor, reflecting pool and bronze vases represent the elements earth, water and fire.

Above: Water runs slowly over the
horizontal edge of the circular reflecting pool that symbolises the sun.
Bronze vases representing the planets
breathe steam and fire.

During the 1970s and 1980s, several recreational options were established
or expanded in the area directly across from the main entrance to the
Tivoli Gardens. As part of this change, it seemed like an obvious idea to
provide a connection between the various functions of the area in the
form of a distinctive new pedestrian axis from Tivoli towards the northwest. Private investors funded the renovation of this public square, primarily the Scala Centre, which houses a number of restaurants and cafes,
a cinema and numerous shops.

The square is designed with a character of great simplicity. The large precisely laid stone floor clearly dominates as it promenades between the
buildings lining two sides of the square. The stone floor is of blocks of light
grey Bornholm granite, supplemented by darker granite bands and chaussé
stone along the facades. The stone floor slopes slightly towards the northeast. The solar system is the decorative motif, with the sun represented by
the large circular reflecting pool of dark granite inlaid with a golden stone
mosaic. The horizontal surface of the reflecting pool emphasises the movement of the slightly sloping stone floor. The nine planets in the solar system are symbolised by nine bronze vases lined in a row on a darker band
along the west side of the square. The vases are decorated with symbols
related to the planets, and the distance between them represents the
distances between the planets in the solar system. There are nozzles in the
tops of the nine vases that emit steam and flames occasionally, adding a
dynamic dimension to the square. Parallel with the line of vases is a single
row of trees, while a four-metre-wide cafe zone on the opposite, sunny side
of the square concludes the furnishing. The simplicity in the design of the
square is underlined by the absence of all the other usual accoutrements:
benches, bicycle racks and signs. Tivoli as well as other squares nearby
offer plenty of seating and other urban furnishings. For this reason the idea
has always been for Axeltorv to project quiet and simplicity. A square for
cafe guests and passers by.

Above: The visual connection between Tivoli
and Axeltorv is reinforced at night. The illumination of the entrance to Tivoli is supplemented by reflections from the pool and gas flames
from the vases on the square.

Left: The solar system is the decorative theme.
The circular reflecting pool symbolises the sun,
and the nine bronze vases the planets. The
vases breathe steam and fire day and night,
adding a dynamic, fairy-tale dimension.

Sankt Hans Torv

Copenhagen, Denmark. 1993
Landscape architect: Sven-Ingvar Andersson
Artist: Jørgen Haugen Sørensen

Location: District outside the city centre
Type: Recreational square
History: Renovated public space
Architectural feature: Surface treatment

*Despite the open character of the site and many traffic arteries,
simple tools turned Sankt Hans Torv into a lively and well functioning urban square. The slightly convex granite floor gives a soft
landscape-like quality to the square.*

Copenhagen
1:100,000

Sankt Hans Torv
1:5,000

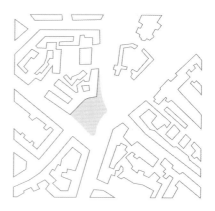

Pedestrian zone 1,800 m²
1:5,000

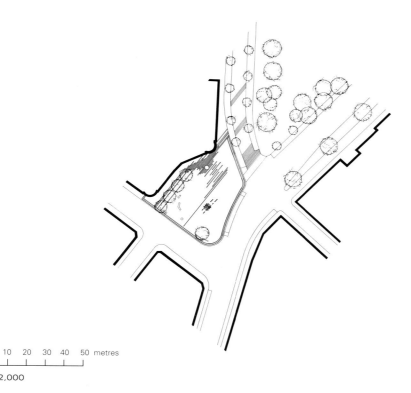

N

10   20   30   40   50 metres

1:2,000

The sculpture, entitled "the house of rain", is in the middle of the square. The surface buckles and forms a depression around the sculpture, giving even more emphasis to its gravity. The tree on the right stands on a slight rise in the terrain.

Sankt Hans Torv is a square in one of the dense urban quarters, Nørre-bro, built outside the old city centre after the city walls were torn down towards the end of the 19th century. Three of the sides of the square are ringed by four- and five-storey buildings containing local shops, restaurants and cafes on ground floor level. The fourth side of the square opens towards a church, which stands free on a triangle that has the character of a park.

In converting Sankt Hans Torv from its old function as a busy intersection to its new function as a square for recreational activity, much of the surface traffic was diverted. This created a new city space with its back against the buildings on the northeast side of the square. The space still has heavy traffic along its southeast side, but a lively city life has grown up around the cafes and fountain on the sunny car-free side of the square.

The surface of Sankt Hans Torv buckles slightly, as if the landscape just beneath the city continues to rise and fall. The one lone tree that was on the square originally kept its accustomed spot, but today stands on a slight elevation, while the very large and distinctive granite sculpture is solidly planted in a recess that marks the point of gravity for the square. The sculpture, entitled "the house of rain", is part of a fountain whose jets of water rise from the floor in varying strengths and splash back into the recess. It is a petrified landscape that finds its own place in the midst of the cobblestone streets that connect the city. The edges of the surface along the streets have also been softened. Rows of linear stone bands that interact with the strong directionality of the sculpture add a dynamic aspect to the otherwise low-key mood of the square.

The cafes spread along one side of the square, where a row of linden trees soften the edge of the square from their position in a rectangular field of gravel. In a corner is one of the city's old kiosks, today used for outdoor food service. A tall slender mast with a gilt top stands like a

giant darning needle and turns a series of spotlights on the floor at night. The renovation of Sankt Hans Torv is an interesting example of how a well designed public space can act as a catalyst for the renovation of a whole district. The design of the square marks a change in the status of the neighbourhood and symbolises the rebirth of the quarter through its lively use as a local recreational square and meeting place.

Above: The "darning needle", a tall slender mast with a gilt top turns its spotlight on the floor of the square.

Right: Jets of water that spring directly from the pavement attract children of all ages.

Far right: Stripes in the pavement and the position of the sculpture bring a dynamic element to the square.

Overleaf above: Sankt Hans Torv is a lively spot with cafes spilling out on to the square, a popular meeting place, particularly for young people.

Overleaf below from left to right: The square seen from southeast. A summer day during the Copenhagen Jazz Festival. The square is furnished with heavy granite benches.

Ole Bulls Plass

Bergen, Norway. 1993
Architects: CUBUS Architect Group
Artist: Asbjørn Andresen

Location: City centre
Type: Main city square
History: Renovated public space
Architectural feature: Composite character

Ole Bulls Plass or square is named after the composer Ole Bull, but is known affectionately as "the blue stone" by the public. In the middle of this simple square with a stone floor is a powerful stone sculpture with a large blue stone – faced with Azul Bahia – as the dominant element. Offset in relation to the axes of the city and horizontal plane, the sculpture provides the transition between the space of the city and the city itself and surrounding mountains. The stone floor of the square is richly varied within the framework of a selection of local stones.

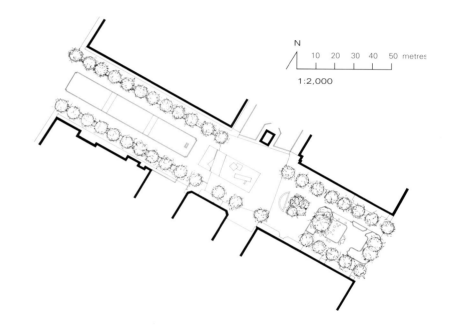

N
10 20 30 40 50 metres
1:2,000

Bergen
1:100,000

Ole Bulls Plass
1:5,000

Area: 7,400 m²
1:5,000

Ole Bulls Plass from the southeast.
On the right, the corner of
Torgalmeningen.

The square seen from the east, with
Ulrikken, Bergen's popular vantage point, in
the background. The stone sculptures
provide cold but nevertheless popular
seating on the square.

In the middle of Bergen, the second largest city in Norway, Ole Bulls Plass is located at the juncture of two of the most important axes of the city, Torgalmeningen on the north-south axis, and the axis from the theatre towards the east. The project to renovate the square is the result of a national architecture competition held in 1990.

The square is designed as a large, simple stone floor from wall to wall. In the midst of the space is sculptor Asbjørn Andresen's "blue stone". The sculptural elements consist of two inclined stone slabs, one of blue stone and the other grey. The stone slabs are offset in relation to the fixed axes of the city and their controlled rotation provides the transition between them.

Bergen's proximity to the sea and the shifting lighting of its coastal climate inspired the use of Azul Bahia, a blue sodalite stone from Brazil, for the larger of the two stones. The extremely expensive blue stone is full of character and has become a town hallmark and an important meeting place. The stone is raised slightly toward the panoramic mountain Ulrikken, while the smaller grey stone is offset slightly in relation to a reflecting pool, suggesting that the entire stone square is floating on an underlying surface of water.

Some of the existing flora in the area, including a small stand of birch, have been incorporated into the new square, which otherwise features very carefully designed stone surfaces. In the middle of the square and parallel to the blue stone is a large quadratic stone field, a patchwork of gneiss and light granite. The stone blocks vary in size and are laid in an arbitrary pattern, although with more of the light granite stone used near the corners. The other surfaces are primarily of red-streaked dark gneiss. All of the stone surfaces feature wide variation in cut and treatment, giving the floor a fine and lively character any day in Bergen, wet or dry.

With the exception of the blue Brazilian stone, local stone is used for the rest of the square. Wide variation in surface treatment and the colour of the stones give the floor depth and character, particularly when wet.

Right: The blue stone and the grey. Water is visible beneath the grey stone, suggesting an underground reflecting pool beneath the stony surface.

Below: East of the stone sculpture the surface is of red-streaked dark gneiss, which adds a dramatic dimension to the stone floor.

Gustav Adolfs Torg

Malmö, Sweden. 1997
Landscape architect: Sven-Ingvar Andersson
Architect: Ib Rasmussen (pavilion buildings)
Artist: Sivert Lindblom

Location: City centre
Type: Traffic and recreational square
History: Renovated public space
Architectural feature: Composite character

The renovation of Gustav Adolfs Torg features circles, ovals and straight lines that inscribe the old trees on the square and control the slight slope of the floor. This urban space, an important connection in the pedestrian network of the city, is both a square and a park and a bus terminal.

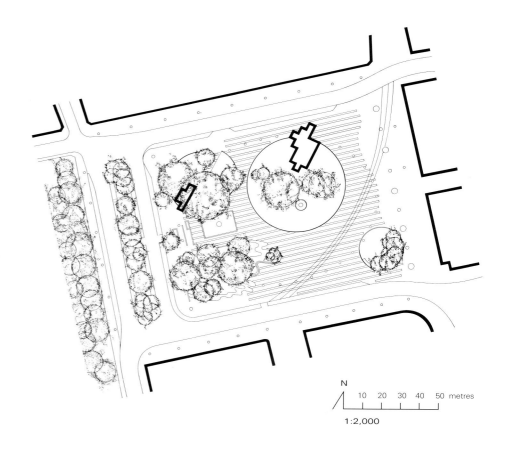

N
10 20 30 40 50 metres

1:2,000

Malmö
1:100,000

Gustav Adolfs Torg
1:5,000

Pedestrian zone: 14,400 m²
1:5,000

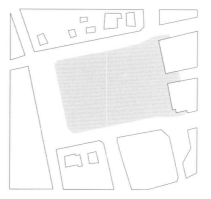

The granite floor weaves its way between the large
groups of trees that give the public space its green
character, providing access from all sides. A curved
line in the floor marks the connection between the
city's two major pedestrian areas.

Malmö has 250,000 inhabitants and is located in southern Sweden, linked by a 20 km bridge and tunnel to Copenhagen in Denmark. The city has its roots in the Middle Ages, the centre surrounded by a canal that used to be part of the old fortifications.

Gustav Adolfs Torg was created in connection with an expansion of the city outside the former walls. Toward the end of the 19th century, the square took on park-like features with a large planted oval of trees and winding paths. Later different sorts of public transportation and cars started to dominate the square. Several bus and tram lines cut through the square before renovation.

Today Gustav Adolfs Torg has a strong green character and is used as a marketplace as well as a stage for changing events. It is a connective link between the city's most important pedestrian streets and the vital traffic hub for a number of bus lines.

Landscape architect Sven-Ingvar Andersson renovated the square by reworking the terrain and by weaving hard surfaces between the green elements. The hard surfaces form a square with lively pedestrian traffic that moves in a slight curve over the square.

The softer elements are groups of grassy or gravelled islands containing large old trees and providing a quieter recreational area. Groups of trees new and old are encircled by bands of granite that also serve as secondary seating. In the southwest corner a surprising serpentine bench borders a group of trees.

The floor of the square has a southern inclination that is visible where it meets the precise granite borders of the green islands. The chaussé stone surface of the floor has regular stripes of granite slabs, which provide a visual scale. A wide curve across the stripes on the surface marks the connection between the city's two pedestrian areas.

Upright granite walls at seat height relieve the circular movements towards the west where the square meets the waiting area for bus passengers.

Above: Pedestrians move in a lively stream past several new fountains erected along the east side of the square. In the background on the right is a permanent pavilion with a cafe and outdoor service, while the other booths change with the various events held during the year.

Right: The surface slants slightly towards the south across the regular horizontal stripes of the floor.

Far right: Along the western edge by the bus stops, linear granite plinths for seating contrast with the circular design of the square.

The largest circle holds a pavilion with a cafe offering outdoor service. Along the eastern facade of the square are several fountains designed by Sivert Lindblom. The lighting for the square forms a large unifying oval figure that moves between the various parts of the square.

The lively design of the square provides a wealth of recreational options. The passer-by can sit and watch the ever-changing stream of pedestrians, find a quiet spot under the trees, lie on the grass or pull up a chair at a cafe and enjoy the view and chance performances of street musicians.

Left: The primarily green character of the city space dominates the central area around the old fountain.

Upper right: The low granite borders offer fine opportunities to enjoy the sun and watch the stream of people go by.

Right: Bordered by a beech hedge, a long bench winds its way towards the southwest corner.

Main street in Kouvola,"Manski"

Kouvola, Finland. 1998
Architects: Mikko Heikkilä Oy and Erkki Korhonen
Artists: Johanne Rope and Juhani Salmenperä

Location: City centre
Type: Main street/promenade
History: Renovated public space
Architectural feature: Surface treatment/emphasis of linear course

Many of Europe's smaller towns are working carefully with the design of public spaces. The main street of Kouvola, a small provincial town in southeast Finland, is a good example. The street space has a simple, robust character that reflects the Finnish landscape and high Nordic skies. The dramatic contrast between the bright summers and dark snowy winters is emphasised in this urban space project.

Kouvola
1:100,000

Manski
1:5,000

Pedestrian zone
1:5,000

N

10 20 30 40 50 metres

1:2,000

Kouvola is a small town of 32,000 inhabitants in southeast Finland, centred in a region with a total population of 100,000 people. The town is fairly modern with a rectangular grid pattern, and most buildings date from the period after the Second World War. Being a young town, the streets of Kouvola are designed to accommodate the needs of modern car traffic even in the centre.

The main street, Kauppalankatu, 26 metres wide, was transformed into a pedestrian street called "Manski" in 1995, and was officially opened after being refurbished in 1998. The pedestrian area is slated for further expansion in the years ahead.

A town without a waterfront, Kouvola chose water as the main theme for its pedestrian street. The street has three different sculptural elements related to the water theme: the map stone, the delta and the rain stones. The elements are connected by an artificial channel of water (length: 150 m, width: 25 cm). The map stone, sculpted in Finnish granite, symbolises the origins of the water from the local river Kymi.

Manski street was repaved and furnished with new elements in 1998. All the furniture, from benches, lighting, bike racks, tree stands and litter bins, was specially designed based on the principle that each city deserves its own distinctive street furniture in order to celebrate local identity. The pavement is composed of grey concrete blocks, and red and black granite. Each functional zone runs the length of the street, emphasising its linear character, and is marked by a different stone surface and texture. The functional approach still leaves plenty of room for pedestrian use and social activities.

The little river in the street starts with the "map stone" and ends 150 m later with the "rain stones", six monolithic blocks of black granite. Small water pipes at the top of these stones allow a constant stream of water to seep down over the polished granite surfaces. The water makes the gran-

Water is the ongoing theme for the street. Above, the map stone with its story about the origins of the Kymi River. Below the 150-metre channel that connects the map stone with the rain stones shown here on the immediate left.

ite come alive with more intensity of colour and adds a soft refreshing voice to the area. Although quite narrow, the little channel of water is a strong architectural element in the street. There is underwater lighting and small stone bridges across the stream in front of busy shops. The platform of the stream is raised 2 cm above the street surface for easier recognition by the handicapped. One of the design goals was to make the street attractive to children. The flowing water in the streetscape serves this purpose very nicely.

The smooth surface of the linear pavement alongside the little stream accommodates changing functions such as parades, fashion shows, and flower exhibitions.

The conditions and the image of the street change dramatically in winter. The water is turned off and its course covered by plywood boards – and snow. During this long, dark season, artificial light is the main source of lighting for most of the day. The lighting is designed to form decorative patterns in the snow, and various furniture elements such as the canopies have some built-in light features as well. Winter is not only dark but cold, with temperatures from zero to -20 degrees C. Snow blankets the surfaces and brilliantly reflects the light from the various street lamps, lending quite a special atmosphere to the wintry street scene.

In the winter the lights and reflections from the snow cast their spell on the streetscape. Light fixtures, like the rest of the street furniture, were specially designed for this project.

111

Broadgate Arena

London, England. 1985-90
Architects: Arup Associates

Location: City centre
Type: Recreational square in private office complex
History: New public space
Architectural feature: Combined square and building design

Broadgate Arena was created in conjunction with a large private office complex in central London. What makes this city space special is its design with a circular stage as the focal point. The stage is ringed by a cylindrical space edged by balconies and is used for various activities both summer and winter.

1:2,000

London
1:200,000

Broadgate Arena
1:5,000

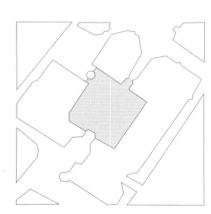

Arena area: 5,900 m²
1:5,000

The arena is converted into an ice skating rink in the winter. Skaters liven up the space and attract a few spectators.

Above: In the summer Broadgate
Arena is a stage for concerts and
other types of entertainment. In
the winter the stage becomes an
ice skating rink.

In the City of London are the headquarters of numerous major financial
and insurance companies and it is here that Broadgate Arena was built
as an integral part of a new office complex near Liverpool Street Station.
The office buildings are 10-12 storeys high and designed to clearly define
the internal rectangular courtyard space that connects to the surrounding
streets and the station through a shopping arcade. There is access to the
lobbies of the large office complexes from the internal space. Broadgate
Arena is the core space in the complex and, particularly in the summer,
serves as a large open canteen for the many employees who work in the
surrounding offices.

The space was intended and designed as a site for performances and
happenings, a public theatre, an arena. The design is reminiscent of the
circular stage and cylindrical balconies of Shakespeare's Globe Theatre.
The summer features changing entertainment with musicians and
theatre performances as well as cafe life. In the winter the arena is converted into an ice skating rink.

The arena itself is a precision-cut circle surrounded by a planted cylindrical "screen", a round space inside the square formed by the facades of
the office buildings. The arena is raised half a storey above the surrounding floor. The main activities are collected within the "screen"' around
the arena, and live their own life with shops on the lower floor and terraced cafes with panoramic views on several levels up against the
screen. The spaces between the screen and the office buildings serve as
circulation areas for the many office people going to and from work, but
they are rather empty at other times of the day. Under the shadow of the
terraces are several stone benches, their use limited to the summer
months.

Fine materials were used to build Broadgate Arena and the surrounding
public space. The floor is executed in dark brown granite and light travertine, and the facades are also faced with a dark, warm stone covering.

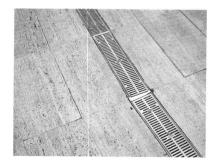

Far left: At lunch time employees
from the surrounding office buildings populate the inner ring.

Left: The floor and other details of
the arena are executed in fine materials: bronze and travertine. The
floor outside the screen is granite.

The area is kept spotless and is monitored by private security guards who keep an eye on the public space from a small circular building that separates the arena from the neighbouring green space.

Not too many passers-by frequent the place, which livens up during the hours that office personnel fill the space or in conjunction with special arrangements in the arena. The "screen" also effectively discourages people on the outside from entering and livening up the space once the 25,000 employees from the office complex have gone home.

Below: People circulate in the area between the circular screen and the rectangular space. Here they have access to the various office buildings and a peek into the inner space of the arena.

Right: The inside of the arena is primarily a stage and recreational area.

Schouwburgplein

Rotterdam, The Netherlands. 1997
Architect: Adriaan Geuze, West 8

Location: City centre
Type: Main city square/urban stage
History: Renovated public space
Architectural feature: Surface and elements

Schouwburgplein is a refreshing example of a radical interpretation of city space surrounded by modern buildings. A large urban stage with an unusual choice of floor surfaces. Another interesting feature is that users can change the lighting.

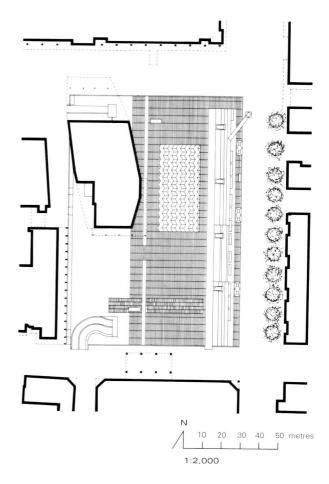

N

10 20 30 40 50 metres

1:2,000

Rotterdam
1:100,000

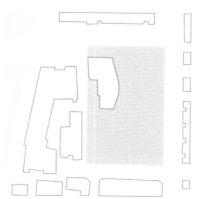

Schouwburgplein
1:5,000

Main pedestrian area: 10,800 m²
1:5,000

At night the square seems to float like an enchanted urban stage, with passers-by playing a dual role as actors and spectators.

Rotterdam is situated in southern Holland and has more than a million inhabitants. It is a busy industrial city with the world's largest harbour, Europort. Savagely bombed at the beginning of the Second World War, after massive rebuilding Rotterdam is now a very modern city with a core strongly defined by the tenets of modernism. High-rise buildings and relatively weakly defined public spaces are interspersed with lower square buildings along broad streets. Schouwburgplein is in the middle of the city, close to the railway station and the famous Lijnbahn, which was the first post-war shopping area in a city centre planned as a car-free zone. The buildings around the square are cohesive in their modern design language and yet have the spatial feel of a collage. As you walk down the street, the changes in height of surrounding buildings and open space provide a mixed urban picture in which the square becomes a stage on which the urban collage is played. In design the space is rectangular and limited, but from eye height it appears as a mixed silhouette of residential and office high-rises, with lower buildings in the foreground housing theatre, music and cinema. A main public space, Schouwburgplein is a place for culture and modern urban recreation, framed by buildings with active, open facades that contain shops, entrances to various amusements and a large number of sidewalk cafes.

The square serves as a large urban foyer for the cultural institutions surrounding it. The city's concert hall, De Doelen, is on the north side, while the city's theatre, Schouwburg, which lent its name to the square, is towards the south. On the east and west the square is flanked by shopping and office areas, while the newest building, a large cinema complex called Bioscoop that allows the square to glide under it, is centrally placed. The building is large and closed, but with a semi-transparent, milky white facade that shines like a translucent skin at night.

Above: To the left are the tall, crane-like light masts. To the right, the cinema, Bioscoop, with Schouwburg theatre in the background.

Right: The square dramatically changes character at night, with the large floor spotlighted by the light masts.

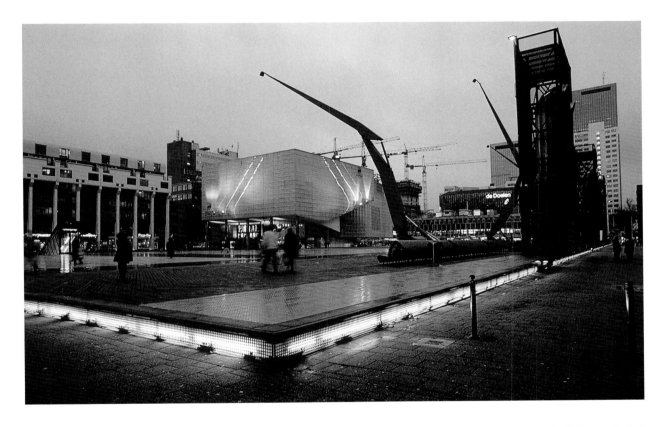

Above: The edge of the raised floor is illuminated from the inside and the space seems to float. Putting a raised deck in the middle of the square makes access difficult for some people, although there are steps and ramps here and there.

Above: The ventilation towers have digital displays that show the time.

Left: Stairs lead to the underground car park through the triangular glass prisms. Light underneath the steel grating is just visible in the foreground.

119

Schouwburgplein also serves as the city's large foyer or stage for people arriving by car, and they can walk directly from the underground car park through triangular glass prisms and onto the square. West 8's renewal of the square was based on the city's open, modern industrial features, which were emphasised by clearly industrial design language, coupled with the use of untraditional materials and construction. The main elements of the square are a large rectangular deck divided into fields by various types of surfacing, four large crane-like light masts and three tall ventilation towers. Together they give the place a raw, unsentimental atmosphere like that of a large ship or drilling platform.

The streets along the square run past the deck, whose large flat surface is raised 35 cm above the surrounding terrain, like a lid over the underground parking area. Darkness reinforces a surreal suggestion of floating: with the edge lit all the way around from the inside, the deck appears to hover above the ground. Various types of surfacing including chequer plate, metal grates, rubber paving and herringbone-pattern wooden decks divide the surface into fields. The lengthwise divisions underline the various zones with their different types of furniture.

Various elements for sitting and leaning are mounted in a linear zone along the sunny side of the square. Towards the east, a railing designed as leaning furniture edges the deck. Here from their slightly elevated position, people can watch passers-by on one side of the street or the large stage above the row of benches further inside the deck. The three large ventilation towers shoot up through the deck at the edge of the stationary zone, which ends in a row of crane-like lighting masts, which users can move by putting a coin in the control panel on the square. Between the kerb zone and the cinema, light metal plates with a small, inlaid rectangular wooden deck cover the centre field of the square.

When you walk across the square, the sound picture changes from the metallic clink of chequer plate to the soft squish of rubber to the wooden clank of the ship's deck and the ring of metal grating. Finally you reach

Above left: A long row of sculpted wooden benches line the eastern edge of the square.

Below left: The floor of the square is executed in bands of light metal plate, steel grating, black rubber and wooden decks.

the "safe ground" of the epoxy-covered concrete deck on the opposite side of the square. Small silver leaves were embedded in the epoxy originally, but the surface had to be changed later and this little ode to autumn has now disappeared. A band stretches across the southern end of the square, containing small fountains that spray water directly from the metal grates and a stone plate. The original idea was for the design of the river and harbour to be etched into the stone, but this part of the project has not been realised.

At night when the deck is lit by the changing spotlights on the giant cranes, the internal lights of the cinema reduce gravity and the deck itself seems to float above the surface. Then Schouwburgplein looks for all the world like a large urban theatre where anything can happen and the 21st century is indeed well underway.

Above: Along the east side the square is edged by steel furniture in the form of a ship's railing.

Left: On a sunny afternoon the benches provide a fine view of the activities on the square.

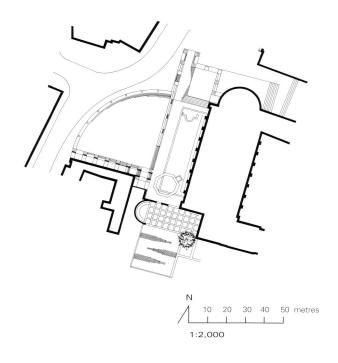

Konstantinplatz

Trier, Germany. 1986
Architect: Oswald Mathias Ungers

Location: City centre
Type: Forecourt/monumental square
History: Renovated public space and new arcade
Architectural feature: Surface treatment

The addition of a single low building in the form of an arcade and the precise geometric treatment of surfaces presents Konstantinplatz with spacious clarity. The floor also bears witness to the long history of the site.

N
10 20 30 40 50 metres

1:2,000

Trier
1:100,000

Konstantinplatz
1:5,000

Pedestrian zone: 4,900m²
1:5,000

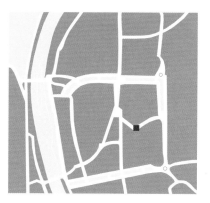

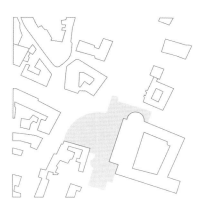

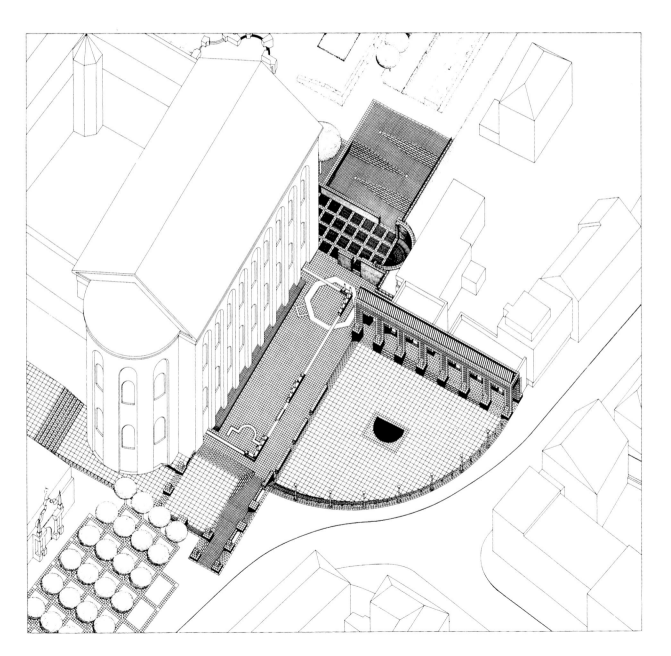

Left: Oblique drawing showing Konstantinplatz and surrounding buildings. Left, the Roman basilica, on the right, the new arcade with cafe and information office. The palace gardens are suggested in the background.

Trier has about 100,000 inhabitants and is located in the German state of Rheinland-Pfalz, close to the border to Luxembourg. The Roman Emperor Augustus founded the town in 15 B.C. and it contains a number of ruins from Roman times, including a city gate, an amphitheatre, the remains of a Roman bathhouse and a basilica, Aula Pallatina, which was the throne room in the palace of Constantine the Great.

The well-preserved Roman basilica forms one side of Konstantinplatz, which is located in the middle of the town. With the addition of an arcade and a precise treatment of surfaces, the square serves as a forecourt that provides a worthy entrance to the historic basilica as well as access to the gardens behind. The architect, Oswald Mathias Ungers, used very few elements and a moderate impact to create a space that is strict and precise despite the highly heterogenous building conditions in which he had to work.

On one side is the impressive Roman basilica, while the other is lined by a patchwork of newer buildings without any clear spatial sense. A new arcade with a cafe among other options concludes the row of town houses and, along with the Roman basilica, forms the walls that hold the space together. The third side is a slightly sloping quarter-circle that is lined with a row of distinctive lighting fixtures that create the transition to a larger traffic area.

The square is a kind of funnel that forms a transition between street and park and leads the visitor down a ramp or steps on the way to the palace and the gardens behind. The two axes flank the funnel, one along the basilica and the other through the arcade.

The square has many layers, a kind of architectural "dig" that reveals the many ages of the site, new and old, simultaneously. The outline of former buildings is accentuated in the floor along the lower part of the square by the Roman basilica. The new arcade and the Roman basilica represent an interplay of new and old that spans almost two millennia.

Above left: The arcade, which faces north, forms one wall of the square. Large groups of visitors cross the square every day on their way to the palace gardens.

Left: The semicircular shape of the square is accentuated at night by the lighting along the edge. The Roman basilica forms the backdrop, bathed in a warmer light.

The main floor areas each have their own surface of precision-cut rectangular stone. The slightly sloping surface of the quarter circle is laid with reddish basalt and surrounding surfaces with grey-black basalt.

In the floor along the basilica, the outline of past buildings is depicted by reddish chaussé stone in the dark basalt. The surfaces of the steps and ramps as well as their intersections are all cut in precise geometric shapes.

Above left: The outlines of former buildings are underscored in the surface of the recessed area along the Roman basilica.

Above right: The floor is paved with precise square granite slabs.

Left: The square has no benches but the bases of the cubic light fixtures and many edges provide a good number of secondary seating opportunities.

Bismarckplatz

Heidelberg, Germany. 1988
Architects: Lindinger & Partners
Landscape architects: Günter Nagel and Dagmar Stillger

Location: At the edge of the historic city centre
Type: Traffic square
History: Renovated public space
Architectural feature: Composite character

Bismarckplatz is an example of a simple and pragmatic solution to a mundane space, a traffic square. A floor with a rectangular pattern ties the two components of the space, the hardscape and the landscape.

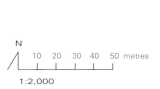

N

10   20   30   40   50 metres

1:2,000

Heidelberg
1:50,000

Bismarckplatz
1:5,000

Central area of the square: 9,800 m²
1:5,000

126

The primary spatial element of the
square is the pedestrian axis lined
by trees, tying the stone floor in
the foreground to the softer forms
of the park behind.

Heidelberg is located in the state of Baden-Württemberg in southwest Germany and has a population of about 140,000. The city is home to Germany's oldest university, which was founded in 1386. From the Middle Ages to the 1700s, Heidelberg was the residence of the palatine counts whose castle lies in ruins on Schlossberg above the town. Today Heidelberg is an active and lively university and commercial town. The city is also a tourist mecca with an old city centre and fine Baroque buildings. Later urban expansion has taken place outside the city's original ramparts, which were levelled in the middle of the 1900s.

Bismarckplatz is a main traffic square located at what was once a rampart between Heidelberg's old medieval city towards the east and later urban expansion towards the west. In the 1870s, the terrain was converted into a park, but it gradually turned into a traffic square as the new urban area towards the west took form. In the 1960s the square was totally dominated by traffic and only a pedestrian island with trees at the northern end gave the slightest hint that the square had once been a city park.

Today the square is an important local and regional traffic hub and links the central parts of the city together. The site continues to be strongly influenced by the many forms of traffic, which include a large number of pedestrians going to and from the various forms of public transportation in addition to vehicular traffic. The main road connection across the Nectar River divides into two dense streams of traffic that run along three of the sides of the square. Bus and tram lines crisscross the square, cutting the rest of the area into a series of fragments. It is remarkable that despite these many divisions, the architects have been able to unite the space into a cohesive pedestrian landscape.

The motivation for the renovation of the square was to create better conditions for pedestrians at this key junction for the public transportation system of the city.

Left: The rows of rectangular white slabs against a dark background form a 12-metre-wide runner that underscores the main direction of the square.

The architectural scheme was to mark an axis in the lengthwise direction of the square from the department store on the southern end to the green park area in the north. The axis ties the green area of the square to the stone floor. The most important features in this design are the surface, a lengthy patterned band that pushes into the green part of the square, and newly planted trees along the sides that encroach on the stone-laid surface of the square from their green bastion.

The other elements on the square, waiting areas, kiosks and lighting, visually underline the axis that ties the many individual elements together. The bus and tram lanes of the public transportation system cut the pedestrian axis. They are marked by a different kind of surface, but out of consideration for the comfort of the pedestrian movement, kept at almost the same level as the rest of the pavement. The other moving traffic is kept outside the pedestrian axis along three edges of the square. Technical devices have been reduced visually by combining them into simple forms or by burying them. The other furnishing elements such as kiosks, waiting areas and benches in the pedestrian landscape are designed to be as transparent as possible and are based on a common design principle.

Above: To make the square as transparent as possible, shelters were designed as freestanding umbrellas, enclosed by large clean glass surfaces where necessary.

Right: The visual variation of passing trams and buses makes for a continuous change of scene along the full length of the pedestrian axis.

129

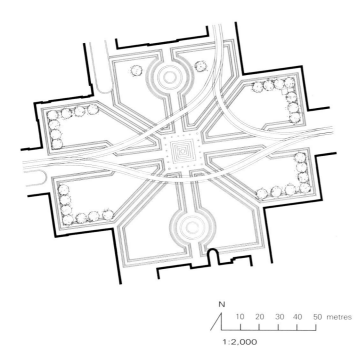

Luisenplatz

Darmstadt, Germany. 1980
Architects: Lindinger & Partners, Hannover

Location: City centre
Type: Traffic square
History: Renovated public space
Architectural feature: Surface treatment

Two contrasting functions are joined at Luisenplatz, the city's main recreational square as well as its most important traffic hub for buses and trams. A strong pattern on the floor that covers the entire space from facade to facade unifies the square.

N
10 20 30 40 50 metres
1:2,000

Darmstadt
1:100,000

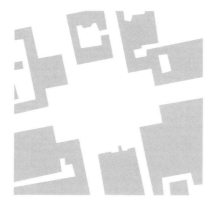

Luisenplatz
1:5,000

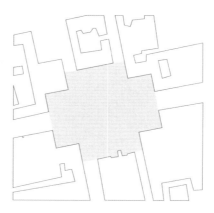

Area: 14,300 m²
1:5,000

Luisenplatz is a large car-free square, with trams and buses moving on the same level as pedestrians. The square is the main junction for public transport as well as one of the most important public meeting places in the city.

131

Luisenplatz is the main square in Darmstadt, which is situated in the middle of Germany, slightly south of Frankfurt. Due to extensive bombing at the end of the Second World War, there are very few original buildings left to tell the story of the centre of the city, with roots extending back to the end of the 1600s.

Luisenplatz stands like a monumental extension of Rheinstrasse, which runs in a symmetrical axis towards the city's castle. The square was created on what was once the revetment of the castle, but has changed appearance and function many times since then. The large column in the middle of the square dates from the 1840s and was paid for by the citizens of the town in honour of Duke Ludwig and the new constitution of 1820. The two large fountains date from the beginning of the 1900s. With the exception of Kollegiengebäude on the northern side of the square, whose facade was almost intact after the bombing, all the buildings around the square are post-WWII. Most of the buildings were erected in the years immediately after the war, in a flat late-modern expression largely devoid of detail and of materials in variations of grey. The dark, almost black, glass facade of Luisencenter, which replaced a bombed manor house on the south side of the square, stands in strong contrast to the rest of the grey framework. The centre was built at the end of the 1970s in conjunction with renovating the square and contains a department store with several storeys of shops, as well as the new Town Hall. With the building of this combination shopping centre and Town Hall, the last empty lot from wartime bombing was filled and the square regained its primary historic shape with axes, symmetrical divisions and characteristic right-angled corners.

Already towards the end of the 1800s, the square began to take on the character of a traffic hub along with the appearance of the first streetcars. Developments in the 1950s and 1960s led to such a heavy increase in car traffic that the city council, after experimenting with partial changes in the traffic pattern, decided to divert all car traffic under the square and thus devote the surface to public transport and pedestrians.

Today Luisenplatz is Darmstadt's main square as well as the city's most important hub for public transport. Almost all of the bus and tram lines meet here. When the square was renovated, emphasis was placed on establishing a good framework for potentially conflicting functions – a large public transportation terminal versus a recreational square for pedestrians.

The red-brick floor is the large uniting surface, with reference to the large column and two fountains of red sandstone that comprise the historic elements of the square. The surface is divided into a large pattern with the help of stripes of white marble, which start at the central column and draw the main axis and symmetrical lines towards it. The in-between surfaces of the floor shift between red and grey granite chaussé stone laid in a peacock pattern.

The functional courses of tram tracks and bus lanes run over and through these precise geometrical lines and patterns. The bus lanes are on the same level as the rest of the square, and indicated only slightly by the surfacing. A limited number of transparent screens to protect people waiting for public transport from the elements stand freely on the floor, with dark blue supports like the lighting masts. Four angled rows of trees along the four corners of the main axis of the square are the main green elements. The surrounding buildings contain shops and cafes that spread into the square with outdoor serving along the edges, while the floor itself is furnished with benches and other places to stop and rest near the fountains.

The square is used all year round as the framework for changing exhibitions, market days and other events. Transparent and airy with large reddish surfaces, the square has its own informal atmosphere that does not appear to be disturbed by the passing buses and trams.

An overall reddish tone unites the floor of the square, with the axes emphasised by red bricks edged in white bands of marble.

Above: Inventory for public transport and lighting are minimal. Windscreens are as transparent and airy as possible and stand freely on the floor.

Left: Relaxed stationary activity on the square is accompanied by the sound of the large fountains.

Left: The focus of the square is the giant Ludwig column set at the junction of the two axes.

Rathausplatz St. Pölten

St. Pölten, Austria. 1995-97
Architect: Boris Podrecca
Lighting: Boris Podrecca and Bartenbach Lichtlabor Innsbruck

Location: City centre
Type: Main square
History: Renovated public space
Architectural feature: Surface treatment

The primary reason for renovating the Town Hall Square in St. Pölten was to establish a large unifying stone surface for fixed or free-standing furniture elements. Variations in the patterns and materials of the surface articulate the floor of the square and describe zones for various functions.
The varied and expressive staging of the lighting provides an important theme in the architectural treatment of the space. Underground parking was built beneath the square, with access from nearby streets.

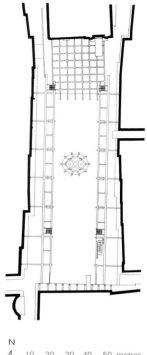

N
10 20 30 40 50 metres

1:2,000

St. Pölten
1:50,000

Rathausplatz St. Pölten
1:5,000

Area: 6,900 m²
1:5,000

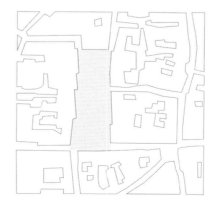

Like so many other main squares in Europe, before renovation the Town Hall Square was used as a car park. Cars are now out of sight in an underground facility with access from side streets. Stairs to the underground parking have been quietly incorporated in the simple furnishings of the square.

St. Pölten, with its 56,000 inhabitants, is located 60 km to the west of Vienna near the Danube River. The Romans called the town Aelium Cetium, while the present name is a reference to St. Hippolitos. The town has been an active trading centre for centuries. In 1986 St. Pölten was selected as the regional capital, subsequently inspiring the extensive building of new administrative buildings and cultural institutions, and the renovation of the city centre. The radical redesign of the main square, the Town Hall Square, was part of this extensive renovation process.

With its narrow winding street patterns, the city centre has the basic character of the Middle Ages. The Town Hall Square, with its large open floor and clear rectangular form, is a distinctive presence in the heart of this structure. Functionally, it is the city's main square and hosts market days, festivals, ceremonies and the many daily events tied to any main square. The long east and west sides are framed by 19th century town houses with shops and residences. Two monumental buildings form the two short sides: the 16th century Town Hall towards the south, and the Baroque Franciscan Church from 1779 towards the north. The middle of the square contains a large sandstone monument, a trinity column erected in 1782.

The renovation of the Town Hall Square, which until 1995 was a large car park, is the result of an architectural competition held in 1994. The terms of the competition requested special focus on lighting. Boris Podrecca together with Bartenbach Lichtlabor carried out the winning project in 1996-97. As is the case for a large number of modern urban squares, an underground car park was built prior to the implementation of the project in 1995. The 148-car facility is one storey deep under the entire square, with access from nearby streets.

The architectural starting point for the design of the square was the desire to create a very simple space with very few furnishing elements, secondary to the large unifying stone floor. The floor is divided into a

The large unifying stone floor is the structuring element of the square. The stone floor is a combination of materials and patterns that describes the functional zones of the square and enlivens the large surface area.

number of longitudinal bands or zones that emphasise and reinforce the main design of the surface. The bands also mark furniture zones and traffic areas. Granite cobblestones have been laid along both long facades, plus an asphalt strip that marks the access for delivery vehicles. On both sides of the strip are bands of grey concrete blocks that mark the furnishing zone of the square. Here are the four staircases leading to the underground parking, the fountain, lighting masts, fixed benches and the outdoor serving area. Thus the entire centre of the square, which is laid with dark and light granite tiles in herringbone pattern, is preserved as a large, open space with a stone floor. The light stone surface of the central square is broken by darker granite in front of the Franciscan Church, indicating the shift between the axes of the square and the church.

The lighting of the square is a significant element in the total architectural composition, and a conscious effort was made to design night lighting that would lend its own architectural quality to the space.

The square has very few furnishing elements, but they are precise designs in carefully selected materials.

137

The floor of the square is lit as well as the facades, emphasising the walls of the space at night. The floor is lit by two rows of high, specially designed light masts situated to emphasise the main direction of the square. Lower down on the masts, four spotlights are aimed at a reflector screen at the top that spreads light over the entire floor without blinding anyone. The lighting level of the square can be regulated by how many of the spotlights on each mast are turned on. Facade lighting utilises the same principle, with spots aimed at reflector screens just under cornices at building corners. The reflector screens send soft, diffuse lighting downward over the facades. Placing the reflectors at corners provides variation and rhythm to the facade lighting, but also gives them a relatively dominating presence due to their size. Having the reflectors high means that the buildings are lit from above at night, just as they are in daylight, while spreading the light so that it does not blind. An important principle in the combined lighting plan is that the reflections from the walls of the space must supplement the lighting, thus providing better definition of people and events in the square.

The light staging of the square varies during the night in step with the rhythms of city life. Both floor and wall lighting are on in the evening, but at 10 p.m. wall lighting is turned off and floor lighting is reduced, providing a considerably lower level of light in the square during the night. In addition to these daily variations, the lighting system allows several different light settings that can be used for various events held at the square during the year.

Lighting is based on reflected light from screens erected on conical steel masts. The light is directed to the reflectors from three lower spotlights. This provides good light diffusion without blinding spectators.

Town fete. Direct lighting on the square is turned off to accentuate the more intimate lighting between booths. Facade lighting defines the space.

Above right: Options for variation are an important part of the lighting program. Light from masts and reflections from facade lighting are only turned on together in the early evening.

Below right: Later in the evening facade lighting is turned off and light from the masts reduced.

Left: The facades are illuminated by soft reflected light from the corners of the buildings. The size and placement of the reflectors raise a number of aestetic questions, and each building has to be considered individually.

139

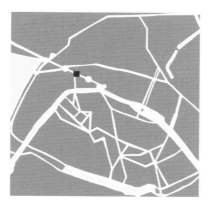

Champs-Élysées
Paris, France. 1992
Architect: Bernard Huet

Location: City centre
Type: Boulevard/promenade
History: Renovated public space
Architectural feature: Surface treatment/emphasis on linear course

With a combined pedestrian area of 47,300 m², the renovation of Champs-Élysées is one of the most comprehensive public space projects in Europe. Doing away with parking lanes made it possible to expand the sidewalks on both sides of the street from 12 to 24 metres. A simple, carefully detailed pavement of grey granite runs the entire length of the promenade, bringing calm and unity to the space. Widening the sidewalks has dramatically expanded city life.

N
10 20 30 40 50 metres
1:2,000

Champs-Élysées
1:20,000

Paris
1:200,000

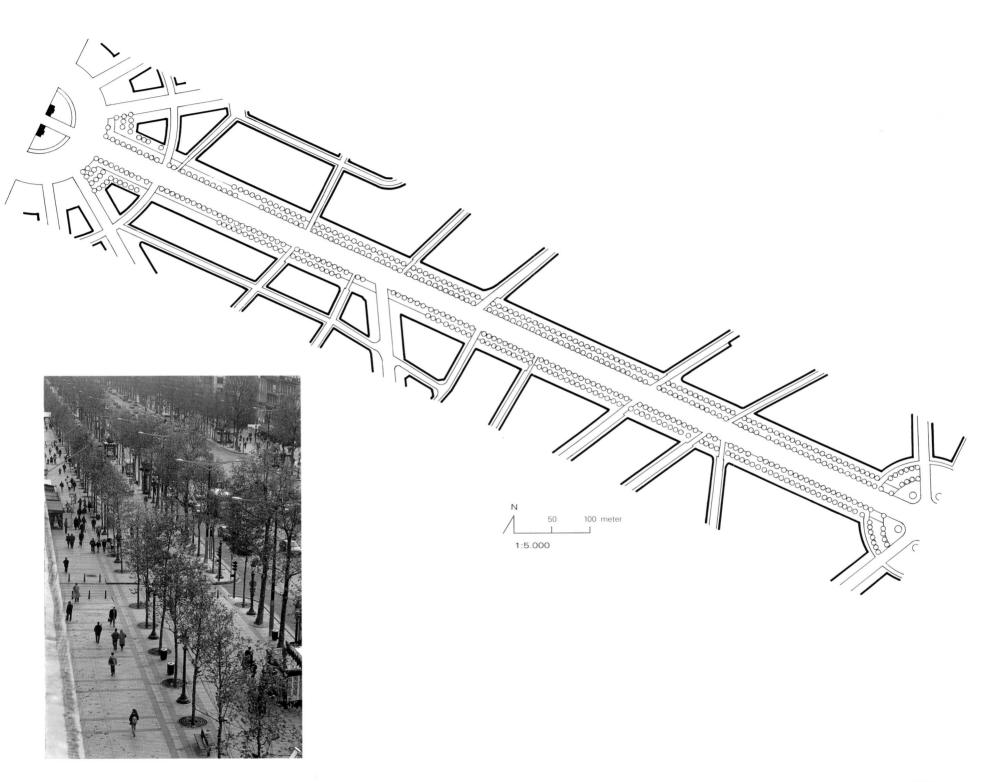

N
50 100 meter
1:5.000

Avenue des Champs-Élysées is 2.1 kilometres long and composed of two street sections. Near the Louvre, trees and park-like landscaping frame the streetscape, but it changes character at Rond Point. In the next section towards the Arch of Triumph, dense 7-8 storey buildings edge the street. The city's most important promenades are here as well, with a rich variety of city functions at ground floor level. The renovation of Champs-Élysées has concentrated on this part of the boulevard, about 1,200 m long. A dramatic improvement in conditions for pedestrians was one key objective of the project. The old access and parking lanes were removed and the sidewalks expanded from 12 to 24 metres on both sides of the street. The street continues to be used for car traffic, ten lanes in fact, and parking has been preserved, but in the form of a five-storey underground facility with room for 850 cars, built under the new sidewalks. Underground parking is accessible from ramps built into the new sidewalks.

The new broad sidewalks are designed with a simple unbroken granite surface that runs the entire length of the boulevard and absorbs the irregularities of the street, and height differences of side streets and underground parking ramps. The sidewalks are paved in a light grey granite, with markings and decorations in a darker shade. The simplicity and elegant detail of the new floors of the city bring a new and much needed dignity to the newly renovated city space. The two sidewalks have a combined area of 47.300 m² in their new guise.

Granite bands mark four lengthwise zones in the sidewalk surfaces. Innermost towards the facades is a function zone, where restaurants can provide glass-enclosed sidewalk service in a five-metre-wide area, while the rest of the zone can be used for open-air service. The second important zone is the pedestrian zone on the new outer sidewalk. The remaining two zones are narrow bands for landscaping, lighting and urban furniture. An extra row of plane trees has been planted between the old and the new sidewalk to supplement the existing row of trees

along the street. Jean-Michel Wilmotte designed the benches and traffic lights as well as the tall, slender, steel lighting masts placed along the street.

Both pedestrians and city life in general have been given a much more dignified and elegant framework along the broad new boulevard sidewalks. It is interesting to note that the new doubly wide sidewalks are often packed with Parisians out enjoying the city, the street and life in general. Twice as much room has made it possible for twice as many people to go for a walk in the middle of Paris.

The space between the facades and the street used to be shared by pedestrians and cars (far left). The sidewalk has now been expanded to twice the width, 24 metres. This generous expanse is reduced in places to allow access to underground parking.

Above: Avenue des Champs-Élysées before renovation, with a single row of trees along each side of the street and parking along the 12-metre-wide sidewalk.

Right: The renovated Avenue des Champs-Élysées with its 24-metre-wide granite sidewalks and double rows of trees, as seen from the Arch of Triumph.

Left: Simplicity and careful detailing characterise the surface of the new sidewalks and street furniture. Granite bands run the length of the entire street. Side streets and driveways are indicated by changes in the pattern of the pavement.

143

Place Vendôme

Paris, France. 1991-92
Architect: Pierre Prunet

Location: City centre
Type: Monumental square
History: Renovated public space
Architectural feature: Surface treatment

Place Vendôme has been given a stylish light granite floor with shiny steel bollards to organise vehicular and pedestrian traffic. Renovation was carried out in connection with establishing a large underground car park, and although the solution is highly contemporary in its choice of materials, it respects the historical traditions of the site.

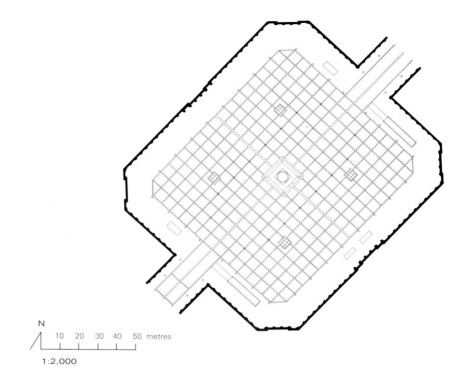

N

10   20   30   40   50 metres

1:2,000

Paris
1:200,000

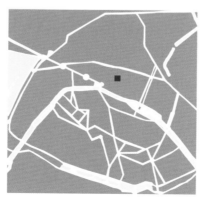

Place Vendôme
1:5,000

Area: 17,750 m²
1:5,000

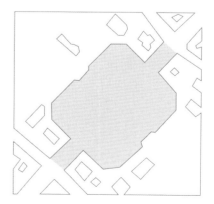

The Vendôme column stands in its accustomed place in the centre but on a new floor. Car access to the individual buildings is along the edge of the square. Through traffic moves on either side of the column and the rest of the space is reserved for pedestrians.

Place Vendôme is located in the first arrondissement in the heart of Paris, only a couple of hundred metres north of the Tuileri Gardens, which mark the start of one of the most important axes in the city, Avenue des Champs Elysées. The square forms a clearly defined space in the dense urban quarter built at the end of the 1600s.

Place Vendôme is one of the classics in the history of urban space design. Originally called Place Louis le Grand, the square was designed by the architect Jules Hardouin-Mansart for the Duke of Vendôme in 1699 as a unified composition of space and building with an equestrian statue of King Louis XIV in the centre. The square was finished in 1701, with the equestrian statue and surrounding facades, but without any buildings behind them. The building sites were subsequently sold and buildings constructed at the behest of the individual builders.

After the French Revolution, the king's statue was removed in 1792, only to be replaced in 1810 by a 44-metre bronze column in memory of Napoleon's victory at Austerlitz in 1805. The column was pulled down during the uprising in 1871 and reinstalled in a reconstructed version in 1875.

In the 20th century the square was used increasingly for driving and parking. In 1972 some of the square was excavated and turned into a car park. With the latest renovation of the square in 1992, the five-level underground car park was expanded to hold 1,549 cars. The new design of the square was carried out under the leadership of architect Pierre Prunet, who is the head of the Paris department for historical monuments.

The main elements of the square were supplied by history, with the Vendôme column in the centre and Hardouin-Mansart's facades as the fixed framework around it. Pierre Prunet's efforts were devoted to reinterpreting the floor, so that it once again provides a large connective surface as a contemporary reflection of Hardouin-Mansart's original idea.

Left: Ramp leading to the underground car park with space for 1,549 cars.

With the exception of the 15-metre-wide sidewalk along the facades, the new floor of the square is on the same level, providing a unified surface of elegant light grey granite. The entire granite surface is divided into large square fields with the help of two different, rectangular stone formats. The division of the surface into squares is created by broader bands laid in a large stone formation, while the surfaces between are laid with small square stones the size of traditional chaussé stones, but cut very precisely.

The surface is fine and even for pedestrians and it is easy for them to get their bearings. Very few elements besides the Vendôme column break the surface. Four entrances to the underground car park are placed symmetrically around the column, but at a respectful distance. In the absence of actual benches, the entrances to the car park serve as a kind of furniture for the square and invite stationary activity.

The degree to which the new overall surface creates an atmosphere of quiet is remarkable now that the cars are regulated and slowed down. With the help of a series of bollards, set in alternating parallel rows the length of the square, it has been possible to indicate where car traffic and pedestrians belong without marking actual lanes on the surface. The short 30-cm steel bollards are placed around the edges of the square and across the surface in a fixed pattern with the taller 60-cm granite bollards, which as a rule stand on the broad granite bands of the surface. The square continues to be lit by classic candelabra street lamps mounted along the edges of the surface devoted to vehicular traffic.

The strict minimalist furnishing of Place Vendôme accentuates its classic elegance.

Right: The walls around the stairs to the underground parking are of the same light granite as the floor of the square and provide the only seating.

Left: Groups of young people enjoy the sun and each other while seated on granite walls around the stairs to underground parking.

Far left: Large 60-cm granite bollards and small 30-cm shiny steel bollards divide the unbroken grey granite floor into a section for pedestrians and one for cars.

Place Kléber

Strasbourg, France. 1993
Architect: Guy Clapot

Location: City centre
Type: Main city square
History: Renovated public space
Architectural feature: Surface treatment

Place Kléber is a European city square rich in tradition. In 1993 the square was renovated as part of Strasbourg's extensive urban renovation program. Two main themes were at work: marketplace and shade. The "marketplace" is a central stone floor on which the changing activities of the city can be staged. The "shade" is an area of deciduous trees in the south part of the square. The stone surfaces are articulated by white sandstone bands that divide the surface and underscore the movement of the space.

Strasbourg
1:100,000

Place Kléber
1:5,000

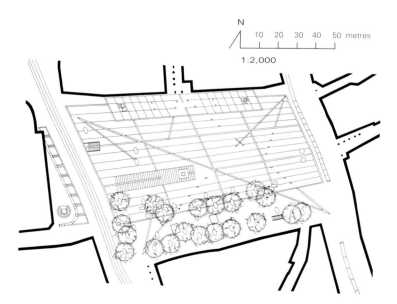

N

10 20 30 40 50 metres

1:2,000

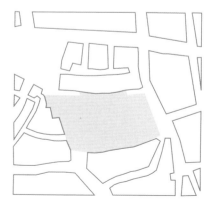

Area: 12,000 m²
1:5,000

Right: Prior to renovation, Place Kléber had traffic on all four sides. In 1992, 50,000 cars drove across the square daily. The ramp to the underground car park was also located on the square itself.

Below: Place Kléber after renovation in 1993. Except for bicycles and the new tram line, the entire square is free from traffic. Stairs and elevators bring pedestrians to and from the underground parking while the access ramps for cars have been moved to the nearby Place de l'Homme de Fer.

Place Kléber is the main city square in Strasbourg, designed originally in 1770 by the architect François Bondel. The large funnel-shaped space is framed by buildings from four to six storeys high. Wide variations in building architecture reflect the dramatic history of the square and the town itself. Heavy modern buildings mix with tall mansard-roof edifices and lower half-timbered constructions, while the entire north facade is occupied by the monumental l'Aubette building, rebuilt after the war damage of 1870, but originally from the 1700s. For centuries, the square has served as a military drilling site, a marketplace and the city square.

In connection with the extensive urban renovation program and the introduction of new tram lines in Strasbourg, an architecture competition for the square was held in 1990. The winning project by architect Guy Clapot combines a large stone surface or "marketplace" with a transparent grouping of trees that shade the south side of the square. The marketplace comprises the entire centre of the square, providing room for the weekly market as well as for many changing events that take place in the course of the year. The marketplace is laid with an urban parquet floor consisting of 70-cm-long, narrow, reddish concrete blocks. A network of white sandstone bands are inlaid in this large stone surface, dividing the square into rectangular fields as well as marking the paths for pedestrians and important entrances. The area for market stalls is also indicated in the floor of the square. Edge zones towards the north and south of the market place have darker surfaces. In the north along the l'Aubette building, rhombic-shaped red granite stones form the floor in the cafe zone. In the south is a grey stone surface under airy leafy trees. This is where most of the furniture of the square is located: Kiosk, stairs, lifts to the underground parking, benches and lighting masts. The square contains many elements and the variation of urban equipment provide the dynamic, almost hectic rhythm that emphasises the position of the square as the active centre of the city.

Pedestrians have free reign over the entire floor of the square. The surface is articulated by the bands of light sandstone inlaid into the grey concrete blocks.

Right: The square is lit by lamp posts with
white glass domes, as well as by six large
masts with adjustable arms and levers. The
light masts are fixed at various angles and
heights.

Below: The pattern of small, grey concrete
blocks is interrupted by oval patches of
dark polished granite and plinths for seating
in the same material.

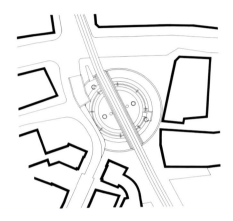

Place de l'Homme de Fer

Strasbourg, France. 1994
Architect: Guy Clapot

Location: City centre
Type: Traffic square
History: Renovated public space
Architectural feature: Surface and elements

Place de l'Homme de Fer is the square where Strasbourg's new tram lines cross. Seen in terms of traffic and function, it is the centre of the city. Its triangular shape and the non-uniform buildings at its edges are countered by the introduction of a new centrally placed design element, a ring-shaped glass roof that rises from a circular pedestrian plateau.

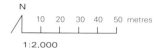

N

10 20 30 40 50 metres

1:2,000

Strasbourg
1:100,000

Place de l'Homme de Fer
1:5,000

Pedestrian zone: 2,000 m²
1:5,000

Place de l'Homme de Fer seen from the west in September 1999. Note the work on the tracks for the new tram line B, to the left behind the large circular glass roof. In the foreground is the ramp to the underground car park under Place Kléber.

Place de l'Homme de Fer is a small triangular urban space, with about 70 metres of facade length. The square arose in connection with rebuilding the city after bomb damage from the Second World War. The east side of the square features older town houses, while modern shops and office buildings line the streets towards north and west.

The renovation of the square together with the Place Kléber project is part of the combined plan for the renovation of the entire area. The introduction of the first new tram line in 1994 and the desire to give the new public transportation system high priority both functionally and visually are the inspiration for renovation. Place de l'Homme de Fer is the tram stop for Place Kléber and thus the main tram station. With the opening of tram line B in the year 2000, the little square is now also the junction for the two main lines in the city. The site also supports other traffic functions such as taxi stands, bicycle parking, and stairs, elevator and ramp to the underground parking facility.

This complex project was approached with a distinctive unifying architectural element, a large ring-shaped glass roof that rises on steel columns from a circular tram stop plateau. The shape of the square and the non-uniform buildings along its edges are countered by the introduction of this new design element that dominates the space.

The outer and inner diameters of the large glass roof are 35 and 20 metres respectively, and it is raised 7,5 metres above the floor. The centrally situated circular tram stop with the "floating" glass roof accentuates the high priority of the stop and the tram line in the cityscape. Here is a traffic hub and the centre of the system. The glass roof also consciously divides the space into layers, with an active lower floor of people, traffic and shops, and shields them from the impression of the non-uniform buildings at the upper storey level. The extensive furnishings of the square have been placed under the large glass roof on the carefully unified stone surfaces of grey, red and white.

Left: Place de l'Homme de Fer seen from the north before and after the renovation of the square. Place Kléber is just visible in the background. The ramp to the underground parking was moved from Place Kléber to Place de l'Homme de Fer in connection with renovating the two squares.

The little square is overwhelming both visually and acoustically with its glass roof, tram lines, furnishing and car traffic to and from the underground car park.

The high priority for public transport is reflected in the treatment of the paving and details of the tram stop. The elevated stop plus the low floor level of the tram ensure that everyone gets on and off safely and comfortably.

Place des Terreaux

Lyon, France. 1994
Architect/Landscape architect: Christian Drevet
Artist: Daniel Buren

Location: City centre
Type: Main square/recreational square
History: Renovated public space
Architectural feature: Surface treatment

Place des Terreaux is distinctive for its surprising use of water and lighting, lovely both day and night. The square is literally a fountain of delight, with 69 jets of water that seem to spring directly from the level floor of the space.

N

10   20   30   40   50 metres

1:2,000

Lyon

1:200,000

Place des Terreaux

1:5,000

Area: 9,800 m²

1:5,000

Nocturnal enchantment. Place des Terreaux takes on an ethereal beauty when all of the tiny fountains with their jets of water are lit from below and the wet reflecting surface mirrors the facades all the way round.

Above: Place des Terreaux is a clearly defined rectangular public space that changes character and mood in keeping with time of day. Sometimes almost dry and empty, other times wet and lively. Illuminated and reflecting at night.

Right: Small cubes for sitting seem to grow right out of the quadratic network along the south side of the square.

Far right: Striped bands divide the floor into quadratic fields.

The old part of Lyon is built on the western ridge of the Saône River, while the commercial streets and cultural institutions of the city are located on the more even ground between the Rhône and Saône in the part of town known as Presq'ile. Place des Terreaux is located in this flatter part of the city, which features the straight streets and uniform buildings of the 1700s. The opera house, Town Hall and several museums are in the quarter near the square.

Place des Terreaux is a large rectangular square surrounded by some of the most significant monuments the city has to offer. Towards the east is the old Town Hall, rebuilt by the architect Jules Hardouin-Mansart after a fire in the 1600s, while the west leads to a shopping area. On the south side is Palais Saint-Pierre, which after renovation at the end of the 1990s now houses one of the largest art museums in France. A more anonymous and uniform facade series lines the north side.

Daniel Buren and Christian Drevet won an architectural competition for the redesign of the square in 1990s. Their design is one of great simplicity, using few elements and a restrained choice of materials. The main elements consist of a new floor divided into squares with small jets of water over the central surface. Towards the south are several plinths for seating near a steel boom that seems to float, marking the boundary to bus traffic. The north side features a row of columns that appear to grow from the pavement, forming the backbone for a large number of cafe chairs and tables that beckon from the sunny side of the square.

The floor of the square is black granite that unites the surface, subdivided into quadratic fields by black and white stripes.

The modules are 5.90-metre fields, which correspond to the distance between columns on the facade of Palais Saint-Pierre on the south side of the square. Water springs directly from jets placed in the middle of these 69 quadrants. When the square was renovated, the existing Berthold fountain was moved from the centre of the Town Hall axis and

Right: The square seen from the east with cafe seating for 950 on the sunny side of the square.

Left: A line of columns defines cafe zone and promenade along the north side of the square.

By day the space is a bubbling oasis with lively pedestrian traffic freely crossing the square between the profusion of small fountains.

turned 90 degrees at its present location in the middle of the north facade of the square.

The renovation of Place des Terreaux includes a large underground car park with space for 730 cars, an element in Lyon's parking strategy designed to reduce surface parking by expanding the capacity of underground parking beneath the renovated squares of the city. Pedestrian access to the car park is discreet through one of the buildings along the square. Car access to parking is from side streets.

Place des Terreaux is an aquatic square. Water from the many small jets that cover almost the entire surface gives the place its special atmosphere. Voices mix with the symphony of splashing water, as scenery and sound change constantly. The large old fountain makes its fixed contribution to the sound picture like the bass or rhythm section of a band, while the many small jets of water vary. Either they murmur en masse, or increase as one in visible and audible crescendo, or rise gradually from one end to the other. The visual scenery shifts constantly to the accompaniment of an equally varied sound picture.

Place des Terreaux is flanked by about 950 cafe chairs with a good view of the aquatic symphony, and serves as a peaceful oasis close to the main streets of the city. During some of the day the square is almost empty and dry. At other times the many cafe chairs are filled with people and the complexity of the site increases dramatically when the many jets of water begin their inventive play. In the evening when the jets are lit from below and the additional lighting of the facades is reflected in the wet floor Place des Terreaux is almost magic.

The many jets of water give the square a playful feeling irresistible to children of all ages.

Place de la Bourse

Lyon, France. 1993
Architect/Landscape architect: Alexandre Chemetoff

Location: City centre
Type: Recreational square
History: Renovated public space
Architectural feature: Surface and green elements

Place de la Bourse is a very small square whose main element is vegetation. The atmosphere is an introverted peacefulness achieved by an intense concentration of trees and shrubs of almost overwhelming proportion.

N

10 20 30 40 50 metres

1:2,000

Lyon
1:200,000

Place de la Bourse
1:5,000

Area: 2,200 m²
1:5,000

An urban oasis. From above only the discreet descent to the underground car park hints that there may be more than meets the eye beneath all that greenery.

Place de la Bourse is in the heart of Lyon, tying the lively shopping street Rue de la République with the quieter Rue de la Bourse. The walls of the square are formed by the impressive 20th century Chamber of Commerce building on one side, and a uniform row of six-storey flats on the other side.

Place de la Bourse is a small square whose wealth of vegetation provides a verdant oasis in the midst of the city. The atmosphere is an introverted peacefulness or urban meditation room right next to the main shopping street. The visitor is immediately enveloped in a green cocoon and the tumult and noise of the nearby city fade into the background.

Seven lengthwise bands planted with maples divide the space, forming a series of small intense spaces on a convincingly intimate scale. More than 100 pots of boxwood spheres line up between the permanent beds, creating small stationary pockets that intensify the feeling of green density. The space quietly leads pedestrians between the two connecting streets, while small verdant pockets tempt them to stop and rest awhile. The length-wise direction of the space is reinforced by alternating bands of two square formats laid in light grey granite. A discreet entrance to one of the city's many underground car parks is located in the middle of the square. Cars have access from the street behind. Like the staircases, access ramps are discreet, with glass partitions that make them almost transparent.

Above: The gentle murmur of a fountain marks the transition from the street to this urban oasis.

Below, left: Precision-cut granite paving is laid in bands throughout the square.

Below, right: Lighting fixtures are embedded in the floor.

Above: Peaceful pockets for sitting
can be glimpsed between the rows
of trimmed, potted boxwood.

Right: Intense green spaces envelop
the visitor.

Place Charles Hernu

Villeurbanne, Lyon, France. 1995
Architects: Charles Bové and Terry Schnadelbach

Location: Outside city centre; transitional space between Lyon and Villeurbanne
Type: Traffic square
History: Renovated public space
Architectural feature: Surface and elements

Place Charles Hernu is a traffic square that marks the transition between two urban areas. Large segments are designated for urban recreation by minimising the area devoted to vehicular traffic in the middle of the square.

Villeurbanne, Lyon
1:200,000

Place Charles Hernu
1:5,000

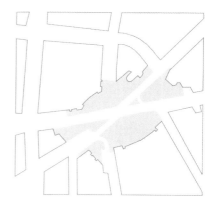

Pedestrian zone
1:5,000

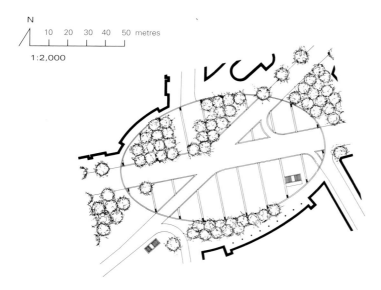

N
10   20   30   40   50 metres
1:2,000

The tall lighting masts mark the edge of
the oval surface, maintaining a simple
spatial form in this mixed space.

Place Charles Hernu is located in the town of Villeurbanne, part of Greater Lyon. Lyon and Villeurbanne have grown together completely and the square marks the transition between them at the meeting of two large traffic arteries, Cours Vitton and Cours Emile Zola. The square is lively and unmistakably urban, flanked by a metro station, several banks, shops, restaurants and sidewalk cafes.

The winners of an architectural competition, Charles Bové from Marseilles and Terry Schnadelbach from New York, designed Place Charles Hernu. The floor is a large ellipse laid with light granite, cut by narrow bands of darker granite to make fields 10.8 metres wide. The streams of traffic disrupt the surface, crossing to form an intersection in the middle of the square. Despite the heavy traffic, large areas, particularly along the buildings, serve as stationary platforms for sidewalk cafes and restaurants. Pedestrians move from "island" to "island" across the flow of vehicular traffic.

The strict geometric form of the floor is softened by a number of trees planted along the edge as well as in the northeast segment. The buildings vary in height and do not follow the ellipse form all the way round, but the distinctive 12-metre-high light masts help support the main shape of the square. The light masts stand like sentries across from each other and perpendicular to the lengthwise axis of the space, thus forming an obvious portal at the narrowest point and emphasising the character of the square as a transitional link between the two towns. The form of the square is most convincing at night, when the large sculptural light fixtures alone mark an oval presence.

One long cohesive facade echoes the form along one side of the square.

Above: At night the large lighting fixtures look like illuminated banners framing the main form of the square and giving presence to the oval shape.

Far left: Inventory on the square is minimised. Litter bins are incorporated into the bases of the lighting masts.

Left: Small metal bollards and the pedestrian ramp are executed in clear, simple forms.

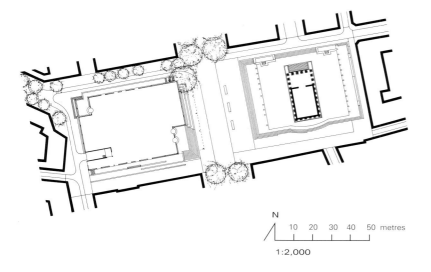

Place Maison Carrée

Nîmes, France. 1993
Architects: Sir Norman Foster & Partners

Location: City centre
Type: Monumental square
History: Renovated public space and new building
Architectural feature: Surface treatment

Place Maison Carrée is a successful example of the renovation of public space in which buildings and new functions have decidedly enriched the site and given it new meaning. The design of the new building and square is clearly contemporary in expression and choice of materials, yet still manages through its proportions to relate to the ancient Roman temple on the site.

N

10 20 30 40 50 metres

1:2,000

Nîmes

1:50,000

Place Maison Carrée

1:5,000

Main pedestrian zone: 4,000 m²

1:5,000

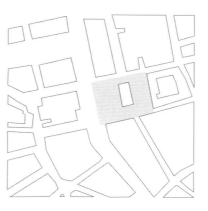

Place Maison Carrée with well-preserved Roman temple in the foreground and the new building, Carrée d'Arts, behind. Two temples in a dialogue stretching over two millennia, framed by a refined cultural square.

With 128,000 inhabitants, Nîmes is the main town in the district of Gard in the south of France, about 100 kilometres north of Marseilles. Nîmes is an old town with many remains from Roman times, including one of the best preserved Roman temples, Maison Carrée, from 15-12 B.C.

The architect Sir Norman Foster renovated Place Maison Carrée, located in the dense core of Nîmes. By building a large new library and art gallery, he redefined and reshaped the square, thus giving it new meaning. Streets lined by shady plane trees lead up to the square, which in daylight stands like a clearing in an urban forest. The Roman temple was originally in the centre of a forum surrounded by columns, which have since disappeared. The temple still occupies its old site on a podium a few steps up from the floor of the ancient forum.

The new floor of the square is several steps higher, leaving the temple on its own and enfolding the new library building that seems to step into the square itself. The new building, which has as many storeys below street-level as above, harmonises with the surrounding buildings in height and dimensions, managing to accentuate rather than dominate the ancient Roman temple.

The library keeps a respectful distance from the temple. Its transparent facade forms a wall along the square, while allowing the floor and the space to continue through and around it to the other side. Each building is made of fine materials representative of its time, the one in marble and the other primarily in glass and steel. Different and yet engaged in a common dialogue, these two temples share the square, each on its own podium.

The floor of local yellow sandstone provides a common framework for both new and old while clearly marking the area for pedestrians. Unity is also underscored by the conscious design of the new building as an interpretation of the form and proportions of the ancient temple.

Far left: Like the Roman temple across from it, Carrée d'Arts rests on a podium that provides plenty of seating in the shadow along the facade.

Left: The new floor unites the large space and surrounds both the ancient Roman temple and the new library and art centre Carrée d'Arts.

Above: The well-preserved temple stands on its own on the square, several steps below the present level of the town. The remains of columns can be seen in the foreground, and the contours of the Roman forum are depicted in the new floor.

Right: The square is spartanly furnished and both the floor and slab benches are made of a local yellow sandstone.

Public spaces in Montpellier

Montpellier, France. 1984
Architect: Ricardo Bofill

Location: New urban quarter close to historic city centre
Type: Monumental square/recreational square
History: New public space
Architectural feature: Combined square and building design

The new quarter, called Antigone, is not only interesting due to its distinctive architectural expression. The unusually large number of ground-floor functions in the buildings collected along the spatial sequence give this new part of town a far livelier character than most corresponding new urban projects.

1. Place du Nombre d'Or
2. Place du Millenaire

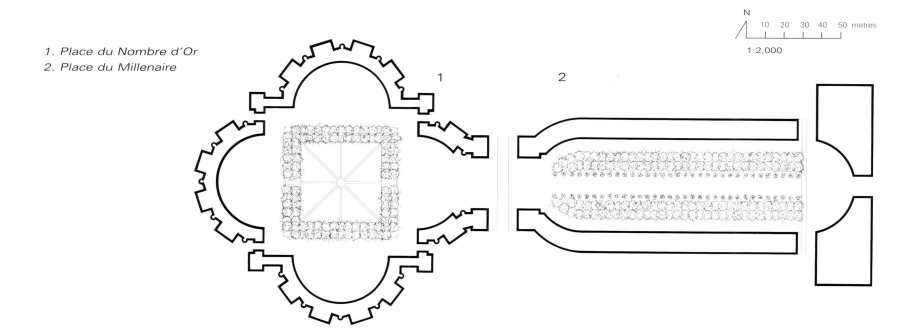

N
10 20 30 40 50 metres
1:2,000

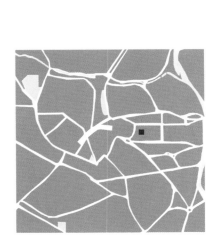

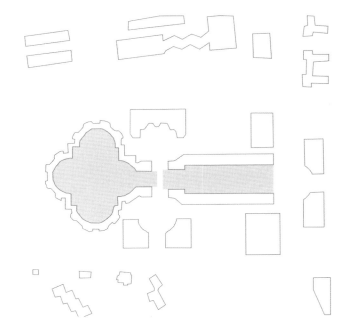

Montpellier
1:50,000

Place du Nombre d'Or/Place du Mellenaire
1:5,000

Place du Nombre d'Or, area: 10,300 m^2
Place du Millenaire, area: 6,700 m^2. Total area: 17,000 m^2
1:5,000

Montpellier is a regional capital with more than 200,000 inhabitants in Herault, located in the south of France near the Mediterranean. The town is old, with a Gothic cathedral and a university founded in 1289. During the 1980s, Montpellier was expanded by the building of an entirely new city district, Antigone. The district is connected via the indoor shopping centre, Polygone, to the old city centre around Place de la Comédie and Esplanade de Charles de Gaulle. The shopping centre and Antigone comprise the eastern leg of the three-prong space that connects the cultural and commercial centres of the town. The new quarter stretches from the city centre over some former industrial and military areas to the river Lez in the east. Here the axis ends at the feet of a monumental building, Hôtel de la Region, on the opposite bank of the river.

Place du Nombre d'Or and Place du Millenaire are the beginning of the central course of space in the new city district. Place de Thessalie and Esplanade de l'Europe are other squares in this large expanse, which forms a fixed neo-Baroque pedestrian axis as an outdoor extension of the inside walkway of the shopping centre. The axis can also be seen as an inversion or negation of the indoor centre's type of space, and the names Polygone and Antigone make reference to this contrast. Lined by buildings seven-storeys high, the axis constitutes the most important public areas that unite the new quarter in its entirety. The buildings are 900 metres long in total and cover 20 hectares. In addition to residences, shops and cafes, the axis also houses a large indoor swimming pool, as well as more regional functions such as Maison des Syndicats, a trade union building.

A new tram line inaugurated in the year 2000 crosses the pedestrian axis between the shopping centre and Place du Nombre d'Or, where a new gateway has been opened to give direct access to the spatial sequence. Place du Nombre d'Or and Place du Millenaire, like the rest of the urban spaces in the axis, have their own character. However, they share a

Above: Place du Nombre d'Or towards the centre of the city.

Middle: Pedestrians coming from the shopping mall walk directly into the axis through the portal.

Below: There is a stop near the axis for Montpellier's new tram line, inaugurated in June 2000.

Right: Outdoor cafe service on the gravel platform under the tree tops at Place du Millenaire.

common trait – strict geometric spaces that engulf the visitor. The transitions between spaces are also precise in design. Place du Nombre d'Or has a floor of concrete stone in warm tones designed as a quadrant framed by trees and rimmed by four semicircular spaces. Tall majestic palms lined the square originally, but they were later replaced with light deciduous trees. Place du Millenaire is a lengthy urban space dominated by large shady conifers planted in gravel surfaces along the sides. The gravel surfaces are used for play and also serve as the platform for outdoor service from a couple of cafes, as well as providing room for relaxing on the benches along the edge of the space. The gravel areas form the transition to the paved edge zone along the buildings. In the middle, a concrete expanse flanked by cypresses tightens the direction of the axis.

Above: Place du Millenaire towards the east.

Left: Place du Nombre d'Or with the central rectangular space framed by trees.

177

Plaça dels Països Catalans

Barcelona, Spain. 1983
Architects: Helio Piñón and Albert Viaplana

Location: District outside historic city centre
Type: Traffic square
History: Renovated public space
Architectural feature: Surface and elements

The surroundings of Plaça dels Països Catalans are very different in character. The space has neither clear edges nor a geometric shape, and the solution for this difficult project shows an interesting break with all preconceptions about public space design.

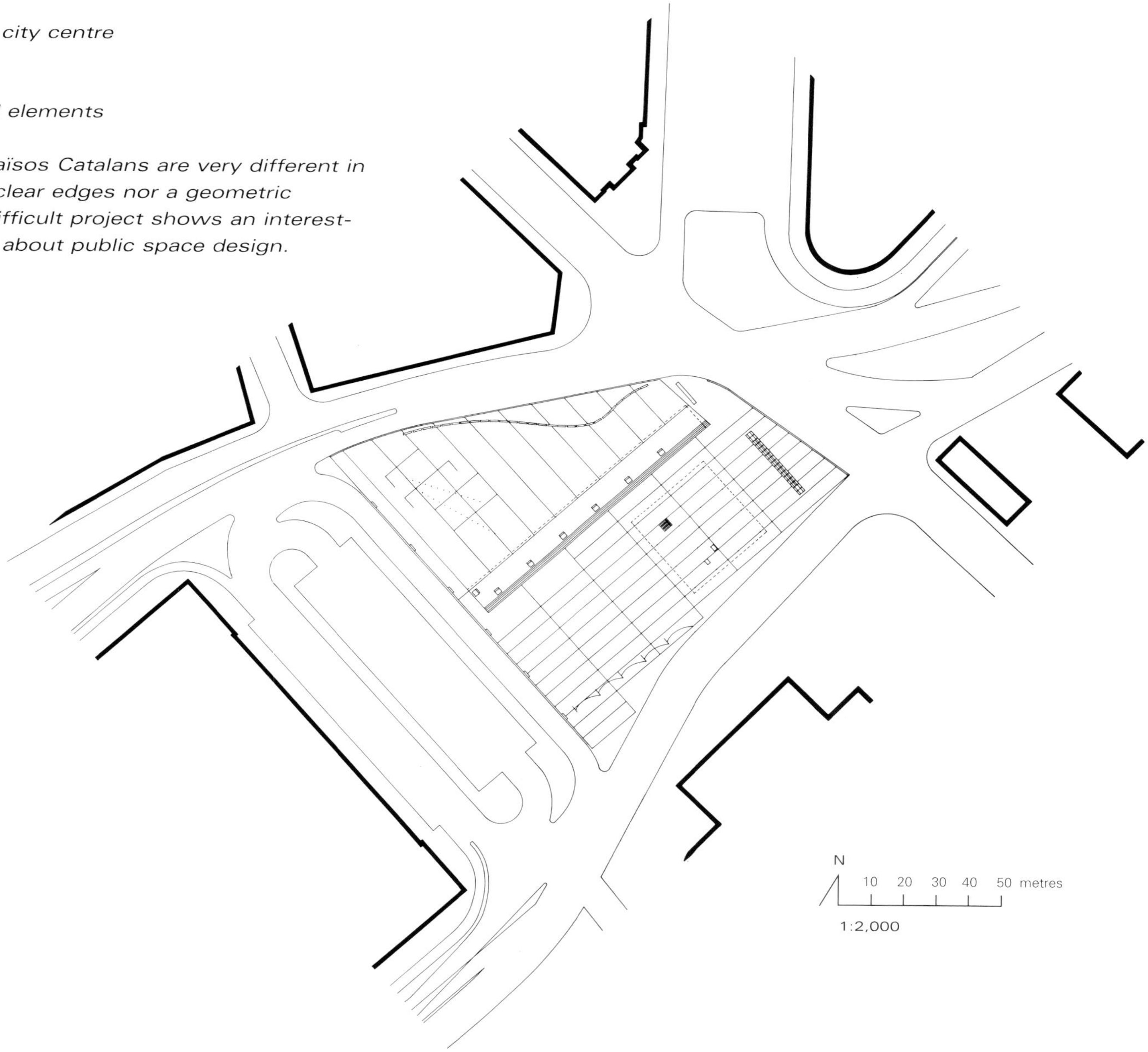

N

10 20 30 40 50 metres

1:2,000

Plaça dels Països Catalans seen from northeast towards Barcelona's main train station. Background left: Parc de l'Espanya Industrial.

Barcelona
1:200,000

Plaça dels Països Catalans
1:5,000

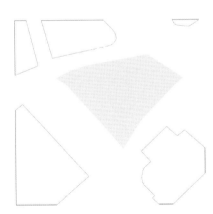

Pedestrian area: 10,400 m²
1:5,000

Above: The spatial elements of the square include a low, undulating roof on a human scale, as well as a tall roof as transition to the scale of the multi-storey buildings.

Right: A special panel with spotlights is mounted diagonally to light the tall roof from below.

Far right: Rows of seating furniture beneath the undulating roof. In the background, the large but relatively low railway station.

Two kilometres west of Barcelona's old city core lies Plaça dels Països Catalans, the forecourt for the city's large train and metro station Barcelona-Sants. The square lies at the junction of two urban structures, where the large grid of the quarter called Eixample meets the irregular but finely meshed network of the Sants quarter in a hub that joins several of the city's large diagonal streets.

The spatial surroundings of Plaça dels Països Catalan are very different in character and the traffic situation complicated, so architects Helio Piñón and Albert Viaplana took on quite a difficult project when they redesigned what had been a large car park in front of the station. The result is a large open floor furnished with light minimalistic metal structures that represent a decisive departure from ordinary expectations about the design of public space. The station is a low, square structure, while surrounding buildings vary from two storeys on one side to six to eight storeys on the other and 20 storeys on the third. In themselves, the buildings do not provide any clear limitation of the space. Streams of traffic surround the irregular floor of the square on all sides, and trains run underneath for almost the entire width.

The floor of the square is covered in light reddish granite. It is slightly humped in the centre, rather like the back of a large animal. There are several metal structures. Uppermost is a perforated metal roof on light columns 15 metres high, marking the first step between the large scale of the surrounding high-rises and the human scale on the floor of the square. The next layer is a lower, lightly suspended metal roof that divides the square into two parts and suggests a direction, an axis, towards the entrance to the station. The curved roof dissipates the feeling of repetition and distance to the station. Many of the square's urban activity options are here under the low roof in the form of granite seating – half bench – half table. A large metal screen with vines forms a kind of wall on the south side of the square toward Parc de l'Espanya Industrial.

In the furthest corner is a 25-metre-long bench of polished black basalt, providing a stationary zone facing the heavily trafficked street as well as direction for the many pedestrians streaming over this side of the square. Smaller elements include a fountain, a row of intertwining seating strips reminiscent of railroad ties and several rows of angled metal bollards which send soft lighting over the surface at night. Lighting for the square is integrated into several of the main elements. A large light well illuminates the expansive roof from below. The curved roof has light fixtures along the edge so that the undulating form is also expressed at night. A series of lighted bollards indicates the location of the most important walkways on the square. The lighting on the square faces an uneven battle with surrounding traffic lighting, however.

Above: The lighting is an integral part of the furnishings of the square. Here the lighting follows the curvature of the roof.

Left: The square has many different details including a fountain, a 25-metre-long bench of polished black basalt and a row of steel balls.

181

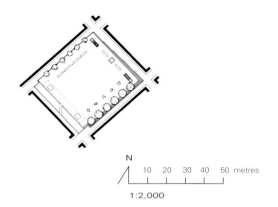

Plaça del Sol

Barcelona, Spain. 1982-85
Architects: J. Bach and G. Mora
Artist: J. Camps

Location: District outside city centre
Type: Recreational square
History: Renovated public space
Architectural feature: Surface treatment

Plaça del Sol is a local urban square showing that a minimal but precise design can result in high utility value for residents.

N

10 20 30 40 50 metres

1:2,000

Barcelona
1:200,000

Plaça del Sol
1:5,000

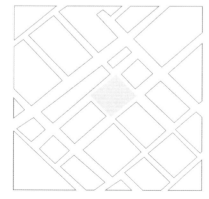

Pedestrian area: 1,700 m²
1:5,000

Plaça del Sol is the neighbourhood sitting room. The men are reading the newspaper or passing the time of day at cafe tables. Mothers and grandmothers knit while keeping one eye on the children playing on the square after school.

Less than two kilometres northwest of the old city centre of Barcelona in the district called Gràcia are a series of small squares, each with its own theme – church square, town hall square, playground – as well as Plaça del Sol, the main square for urban recreation in the neighbourhood. This square is the meeting place and stationary activity magnet for the neighbourhood, and it was renovated on the basis of a proposal from J. Bach and G. Mora, who also designed the renovation of the other squares in this part of the city. Plaça del Sol is located centrally and has shops and cafes in buildings along its edges.

The floor of the square is a sharply cut quadrant in the middle of the space, furnished with very few main elements organised around the mid-axis. Three tall masts with indirect lighting and four benches divide the floor into a furnished edge zone with sidewalk cafes, and an open area for changing activities in the middle of the space. The entrance to an underground car park is hidden behind an airy roof along one edge of the square. Rows of trees shade sidewalk cafes along two sides. The tautness and symmetry of the design seem more relaxed at eye height, mainly because the dominating furnishing elements, lighting masts and benches are placed along one side of the square. A small sculpture in the shape of a sundial is placed at the northeast side of the square.

The greyish stone surfaces of the floor are horizontal to but higher than the surrounding streets, sloping towards the eastern corner where the difference in height between square and street is evened out by several steps.

The floor has a discreet variation of stones laid in bands of various widths, which are again divided in a larger rhythm by smaller bands of stones with a slightly rougher surface, providing a light contrast to the otherwise flat surface. Like the rest of the inventory, the four double benches and three narrow masts with indirect lighting were designed specifically for this square.

Above: The outdoor cafés come to life in the afternoon and the square hums with activity until late in the evening.

Right: The square is a raised horizontal plateau. A row of steps along the southeast corner compensates for the fall in the terrain.

Far right: The simple unifying floor with discreet variation in the size and texture of the stone blocks.

Above: The benches were designed especially for the square.

Middle: The ramp to the underground car park with the little pedestrian bridge crossing the "moat".

Left: The tall light masts provide soft indirectly lighting. Several direct spotlights were added later.

Parc del Clot

Barcelona, Spain. 1988
Architects: Dani Freixes and Vicenc Miranda
Artist: B. Hunt

Location: District outside historic city centre
Type: Recreational square/neighbourhood park
History: New public space
Architectural feature: Composite character

*Parc del Clot is an interesting combination of neighbourhood park
and square. The preservation and reuse of elements from the old
factory buildings on the site give Parc del Clot a special character
and fuel for the imagination.*

N

10 20 30 40 50 metres

1:2,000

Barcelona
1:200,000

Parc del Clot
1:5,000

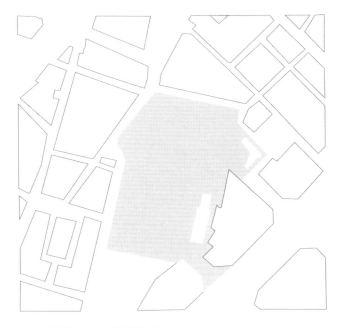

Parc del Clot, area: 29,000 m²
1:5,000

Parc del Clot is divided into two almost
equal parts: In the foreground, the
recessed recreational square, with the
fertile green park in the background.

Parc del Clot lies northeast of Barcelona's old city centre in the part of town known as Sant Marti. It is a park as well as a neighbourhood square, a new place and yet old. A wonderful city space has arisen from the partial demolition and reuse of the brick walls from former factory buildings.

The rectangular form of Parc del Clot sets it apart from the rest of the urban structure of the area, which is marked by the confrontation of the rectangular grid of the city with the large diagonal boulevards. The partially preserved walls create the distinctive rectangular framework that unifies Parc del Clot. The walls define the park, determining what is outside and what is inside and providing glimpses back and forth through the old window openings. Inside this framework, the park has a large number of highly varied components.

Parc del Clot is divided into two main areas: a square with a stone surface that serves as the urban recreation area for the neighbourhood, and a soft, partially green park landscape. The recessed square creates an amphitheatre-like atmosphere and provides seating in the form of a broad staircase cut into the terrain. Two straight pedestrian paths cut diagonally through the park and are carried above the square by light footbridges. The pedestrian paths tie the park to its surroundings both functionally and visually by providing shortcuts over the square. A preserved chimney serves as a landmark that points the way to the staircase connecting the park to the street network of the city a few steps down. Rushing water from a fountain provides an auditory element for the park. The park and square are finely integrated into the local neighbourhood and the varied nature of the combined site attracts nearby residents of all ages.

Parc del Clot creates strong impressions, its old walls suggesting a recreation of architectural archetypes. In one corner is a "Moorish" hall with a reflecting pool and a meditative atmosphere inspired by the cast iron

columns of a former factory. In sharp contrast is another piece of brick wall along the edge of the park reworked into a 25-meter-long "Roman aqueduct", whose thundering cascade of water drops 4-5 metres into a pond. A third wall is reminiscent of a temple ruin atop an acropolis, while a staircase cuts downward into the foundation of the large chimney, once again much like a column from a large temple. Behind the "column" is a wall of Babylonian dimensions. The space is lit by four tall light towers built of glass modules.

Above: The "town wall" and monumental staircase in the northeast corner leading to the green landscape of the park.

Right: The recessed square is used as a playground and platform for changing events.

Middle: The "Moorish" garden and reflecting pool create a meditative mood.

Far right: The wall along the playground on the northern side of Parc del Clot is a backdrop that allows glimpses into the street behind.

Above: The recessed square is a popular recreational area for nearby residents of all ages.

Right: Pedestrian bridges cut diagonally across the recessed square, connecting the park to the rest of the neighbourhood.

Far right: The large "aqueduct" with its cascades of water provides an effective acoustic framework for the square. In the background, a pedestrian bridge cuts through the wall past the waterfall. Behind the waterfall are two of the four large light towers that illuminate the recessed square in the evening.

Plaça del General Moragues

Barcelona, Spain.1988
Architect: Olga Tarrasó
Artist: Elsworth Kelly

Location: District outside historic city centre
Type: Recreational square and neighbourhood playground
History: Renovated public space
Architectural feature: Composite character

Plaça del General Moragues has surfaces that vary widely in character: brick, natural stone, gravel and grass. The unifying element is an architectural composition of triangles that spring from the shape of the square itself.

N

10 20 30 40 50 metres

1:2,000

Barcelona
1:200,000

Plaça del General Moragues
1:5,000

Pedestrian zone, area: 5,500 m²
1:5,000

Plaça del General Moragues from the north. Shown are the main elements of the square: two sculptures, the slightly sloping brick floor, gravel floor and grey granite floor that cut through the middle of the square. Under the trees, a grassy triangle.

Above: As shown here, the edges of the different elements of the square are used most frequently. In the foreground, the brick floor, as well as the edge of the green triangle behind.

Plaça del General Moragues is located three kilometres north of the old city centre of Barcelona in the neighbourhood known as Sant Andreu. The triangular shape of the site is due to the meeting of a large square grid and the railway, which cuts diagonally through the city structure from north to south. Plaça del General Moragues is a local urban square, created on one of the triangles that the railway cut from the characteristic quadratic grid of Barcelona. The square is designed like a puzzle of triangles, overlapping each other to some extent, but each with its own basic character. A large sloping brick surface dominates along one edge, while a green triangle of grass and trees grows on the other. Between these two configurations, a gravel-covered terrace presses its way into the unifying triangle. The gravel surface ends in a broad fortified edge that forms a horizontal bastion along the road that follows the railway. With its railing, the bastion is reminiscent of the compass bridge of a ship, providing a view of the railway grounds and Pont de Felipe II in one direction. In the other direction, people seated on benches can watch children in the playground and admire two sculptures by Elsworth Kelly. The outermost triangle, defined by the facades of the buildings, is lined by trees along the streets. A larger unified field of systematically planted trees overlaps the small triangular grass verge, while smaller groups of trees are planted in both stone and gravel surfaces.

It is along the edges that things happen at this square. A seating strip is installed along the compass bridge, another along the grassy triangle. The raised edges along the brick surface are frequently used as secondary seating options. The sloping brick surface, reminiscent of the Campo in Siena, has a textured feel when lit by the midday sun. In the afternoon shadow the area is irresistible to children with their skateboards and roller-skates.

Left: The slightly sloping brick floor has a distinctive textural quality when it lies almost undisturbed in the heat of the day.

Below left: When afternoon shadows cool down the warm brick floor, it is used for bicycling and skateboarding.

Below: The edge of the square towards the railway station has a long ship's railing that provides back support for the slab benches.

193

Plaça Barange

Granollers, Spain 1986
Architects: Helio Piñón and Albert Viaplana

Location: City centre
Type: Main square
History: Renovated public space
Architectural feature: Surface and elements

Plaça Barange has a number of interesting new interpretations of city space and its elements. The character of the lighting is almost scenographic with great variation in intensity.

N

10 20 30 40 50 metres

1:2,000

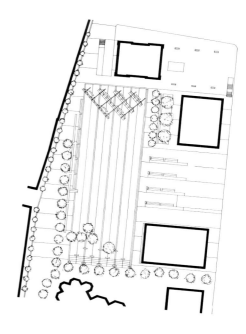

Granollers
1:50,000

Plaça Barange
1:5,000

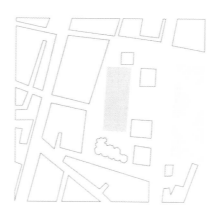

Main pedestrian zone: 3,400 m²
1:5,000

View from the top floor of the
hospital south of the square.
Shown at the end of the rectangular brick floor, the metal
screens that provide shade.
To the left are the benches and
above them the large elongated
lighting fixture.

Granollers is a market town with about 50,000 inhabitants, located 30 km north of Barcelona. Plaça Barange is in the middle of town in a mixed urban neighbourhood. From the square there is a visual connection to a park east of the city centre on the other side of a major traffic artery. The square is surrounded by a wide variety of buildings. Towards the west is a row of traditional two- to four-storey buildings with shops on the ground floor. Towards the east are a couple of lower freestanding buildings along a larger shopping street. The north end has a single low building that houses a post office, while the southern end is dominated by a multi-storey hospital.

The square's most important spatial element is the large rectangular brick floor that connects the space. Laid with red brick between light bands of concrete, the floor is slightly elevated, discreetly suggesting that there is underground parking beneath. The floor is raised like a large saddle at the southern end of the square.

The floor has three distinctive furnishing elements. On the northern end is a series of steel screens that provide shade with seating furniture beneath. A metal sculpture thrusts its way through the middle of the floor, while the southern end has several low semi-circular elements that are part of the lighting for the square. Along the western edge is a distinctive row of benches flanked by a steel construction that supports the elongated lighting fixture for the square. Rows of trees line the edges of the square, while a small group of trees encroaches on the brick floor itself.

The square is a study in light and shadow by day and by night. In the midday sun people can seek shade under the light steel construction at the end of the square. The mood changes in the evening, and the lighting takes on an almost scenographic character. Along one side, a bank of projectors bathes the centre of the square in light, giving children and young people the opportunity to continue their activities in the evening.

At the end toward the hospital, the lighting is positioned low and dimmed. At the opposite end under the screens, a more focused type of lighting illuminates the stationary activity areas. On the curved back of the square, an illuminated metal sculpture breaks through the floor as if sent by messengers from the underworld.

Above: A slab bench under a metal screen with a view of the illuminated sculpture sticking out of the floor of the square.

Far left: Benches run along the edge of the brick floor under the metal supports for the elongated lighting fixture.

Left: The metal screens at the northern end of the square furnish the space and provide shade.

Top: The square is illuminated by varied light intensity and types of lighting fixtures. Foreground, one of the low fixtures that provide dimmed lighting at the southern end of the square. In contrast, the 'lightening rods' on the left provide brilliant light that is dimmed by the metal screens in the background.

Middle: The southern end of the square is quieter with dim, indirect lighting.

Right: The light is more limited at the northern end, directed to the floor by lighting boxes mounted under the supports for the metal screens.

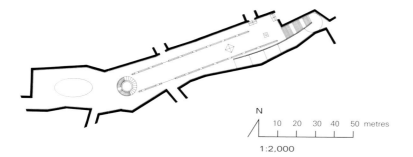

Plaza de Carlos III el Noble

Olite, Spain. 1989
Architect: Francisco Mangado Beloqui

Location: City centre
Type: Main square
History: Renovated public space
Architectural feature: Surface and elements

A town and its history can play a valuable role when city squares are redesigned for contemporary urban life. The square in the little Spanish town of Olite illustrates this combination nicely. It serves as a transit mall, meeting place and stationary activity square, as well as a link between parts of town. The architectural language is simple and precise, with the use of classic architectural forms and elements to decorate and furnish the space.

N
10 20 30 40 50 metres

1:2,000

Olite, Spain
1:50,000

Plaza de Carlos III el Noble
1:5,000

Plaza de Carlos III el Noble,: 2,900m²
1:5,000

Above: View of Olite. The Royal Palace of the Navarran kings is shown in the foreground.

Right: The square is designed using only a few, simple elements. A quiet cohesive stone floor is furnished with simple geometric figures and shapes. The sphere is a fountain, while the pyramid conceals one of the staircases to the underground vaults. The benches emphasise direction and space and define the traffic areas.

Today Olite is a small town of 3000 people, located in the northwest of Spain near Pamplona. In the 14th and 15th centuries, the town was home to the reigning kings of Navarra, and the colourful history of the town is reflected in its buildings from Roman times, the Middle Ages and the Renaissance. Buildings from various periods also provide the framework for the town's long, irregularly shaped main square, Plaza Carlos III.

The eastern end of the square is crowned by the Royal Palace of the Navarran kings, with the modern Town Hall at the opposite end, while the long sides of the square are lined by three- and four-storey buildings from various historical periods. The square is centrally located, and after renovation in 1987, is now free of parked cars and through traffic.

The shape of the square bears traces of the discovery of a system of subterranean medieval vaults thought to be underground passages to the palace. The vaults now house the Tourist Information Office and several exhibition rooms, and their use has necessitated the building of stairways on the new square.

Architecturally, the conversion has been executed with great confidence and simplicity. The space is tied together by a simple stone floor laid with the local Calatorao stone. Several figures and shapes representing classic architectural elements have been inlaid into this simple floor. An oval surface of polished stone has been laid in front of the Town Hall, in order to define an area for meetings and festivities. The entrances to the underground vaults in the middle of the square are executed in steel in the shape of a circle and a pyramid, while the precise block-shaped stone benches underline the direction of the square and define the area for traffic. An alabaster fountain in the shape of a sphere concludes the composition of the square in basic architectural elements. People and activities bring life to this dignified square, which with its simple design language and furnishings creates an atmosphere of calm and quiet in which the history of the site is almost audible.

Above: View from the Town Hall at the western end of the square. In the foreground is the oval ceremonial area; behind is the circular entrance to the underground vaults.

Far right: Under the square are historical passages to the palace. Today the medieval vaults are used for exhibitions and the Tourist Information Office.

Right: The eastern-most staircase to the underground vaults is marked by a precision-cut black steel pyramid.

Right: Plaza Carlos III from the east. In the foreground is the circular stairway to the underground vaults. The square is framed neatly by the marble-faced stone benches.

Left: Furnishing elements are executed in carefully selected materials with the use of a simple, precise design vocabulary.

Piazza Matteotti

Catanzaro, Italy. 1989-91
Architect: Franco Zagari

Location: At the edge of the old city centre
Type: Recreational square and promenade
History: Renovated public space
Architectural feature: Composite character

The square is a connective link between the old city centre
towards the south and the new part of town towards the north.
The design of Piazza Matteotti contains a new and surprising inter-
pretation of urban space. The floor is a large op-art painting and
the square in its entirety a rhythmic urban sculpture.

N
10 20 30 40 50 metres

1:2,000

Catanzaro
1:50,000

Piazza Matteotti
1:5,000

Pedestrian zone: 4,400 m²
1:5,000

Foreground: the promenade edged by a serpentine bench towards the traffic lanes. Background left: the Court House with a small urban park as a forecourt. The modern Grand Hotel is in the background, right.

203

Perched on a naked Calabrian hilltop, Catanzaro is a town with about 100,000 inhabitants in southern Italy. Piazza Matteotti forms a narrow passageway between the old city centre and the newer part of town towards the north. Several important public buildings surround the piazza, the Court House on the north side and a school to the west. To the east are a bank and the Grand Hotel, a modern multi-storey building behind which the terrain falls dramatically.

The new space consists of three parts: promenade, square and urban park. The promenade connects the two parts of town and is located in the middle of Via Indipendenza. The floor is inspired by a Vasarely painting, inlaid with a dancing pattern of light travertine marble blocks on a striped floor of grey and blue-black African granite. At either end of the promenade is a small open pavilion with a flat roof in the same pattern as the floor of the square. Along the traffic lanes on the west side is a row of palms flanked by a length of serpentine stone benches that underscore the elongated fall of the space. There is a second row of curved travertine marble running across the promenade, originally conceived as a connection across the traffic lanes on either side.

The square itself is a smaller space that spreads out slightly between the promenade and the park. It is dominated by a large sundial and a sculptural staircase that gives people a good view of the shadow cast by the sundial or a digital display on the dial. Across from the Court House is an urban park, a small oasis of green with a statue in the symmetrical axis of the building. On the whole the space features delight in design with serpentine curves and wavy lines. A new and surprising interpretation of public space with the floor as a large picture and the place itself as a large urban sculpture.

Above: The floor of the promenade is inspired by an op-art painting by Vasarely with light travertine marble blocks laid on a darker surface of striped African granite.

Right: Detail of the eastern side of the promenade with a couple of plinths for seating.

Top: The original idea was for the wide curved travertine band to continue across the traffic lanes.

Left: The pyramid staircase is intended to provide a good view of the sundial but also gives viewers a good look at the landscape in the background between the Court House and the hotel.

Above: At each end of the promenade is a pavilion with the pattern on its roof mimicking the floor of the square.

Below and right: The serpentine bench marks the edge of the square against the traffic lanes. The floor has recessed lighting fixtures that illuminate the palms.

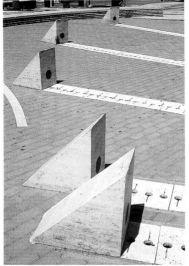

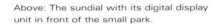

Above: The sundial with its digital display unit in front of the small park.

Left and right: Triangles mark the end of the lines of the sundial in the west, and a series of spheres in the east.

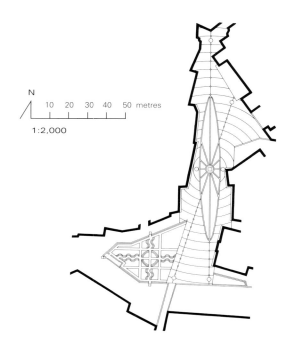

10 20 30 40 50 metres

1:2,000

Piazza Vittorio Emanuele

Santa Severina, Italy. 1980
Architect: Alessandro Anselmi and Guiseppe Pantanè

Location: City centre
Type: Main city square
History: Renovated public space
Architectural feature: Surface treatment

*The main square in Santa Severina is a fine example of a design
that quietly maintains its overall integrity while telling a story in the
intricate detail of the floor.*

Santa Severina
1:50,000

Piazza Vittorio Emanuele
1:5,000

Area: 4,500 m²
1:5,000

The square in Santa Severina seen from the church tower with the 12th century castle in the background. The edge of the park is just visible to the right of the castle gate.

In Calabria in the south of Italy, the quiet little town of Santa Severina lies on a dramatic hilltop. The town is old and boasts a 12th century castle and a church with a Byzantine christening chapel. The main square, Piazza Vittorio Emanuele, known as the Campo for short, lies between the town's two major monuments, the church and the castle. The square is irregular in shape and crammed between the few buildings that the hilltop allows. The square has a closed character despite the relatively large openings at both ends. Because of the hilltop location, these openings provide dramatic panoramic views of the landscape below.

In 1980 the public space was renovated by the co-operative efforts of architects Alessandro Anselmi from Rome and Guiseppe Pantanè from Santa Severina. Together the architects gave the space a fine floor and created a clear division between the two main characters: square and urban park.

The square is unified by a simple floor of dark porphyry chaussé stone from wall to wall. The elliptical figure in the floor is the true unifying element for the irregular space. Several travertine marble circles are inlaid in the dark floor, reaching the farthest corners like rings in water. In the centre of the circle is a wind wheel stretched into an ellipse that indicates the north-south direction and the four corners of the world. A second axis that runs as a white line from door to door connects the castle and the church. The figures on the wind wheel indicate the most important wind directions, while several alchemist signs are reproduced at the junctions of the axes and circles. The circular travertine fields at the end of the north-south axis contain the sign for time, the four seasons and the four rhythms of the calendar: day, week, month and year.

Corresponding fields conclude the axis between the church and the castle with the sign for gold, silver, mercury, copper and iron. The sun, earth and moon and the other planets are also represented by signs in small square fields.

The square with the church in the background. The wind wheel is shown in the foreground. The eye of wisdom is in the middle of this geometric composition.

The design of the square unites great simplicity with the many details that allow pedestrians to discover and enjoy the narration on the floor. The references to alchemy and the cosmos are united in the eye of wisdom, which is at the centre of the composition.

The small park is a bastion between the town and the castle, providing a fantastic view of the landscape towards the west. At the opposite end is a smaller bastion with stone benches along the edge, and a corresponding view towards the east. A deep moat divides town and castle in the south. Towards the north is the church, with its tower providing a counterweight to the solidity of the castle. The park is a sophisticated folly using few materials in a form reminiscent of a Renaissance garden. Strict stone paths divide nine regular fields. From the centre of the park, a circle around a metal solar sculpture, serpentine stone benches wind their way between the trees. Piazza Vittorio Emanuele looks inward and outward in perfect harmony.

Above: The urban park with its magnificent view of the landscape in the background.

Below: Symbols for the planets, metals and wind directions are inlaid in the floor of the square.

211

Public spaces in Gibellina

Gibellina, Italy. 1990
Architects: Franco Purini and Laura Thermes

Location: Centre of new town
Type: Monumental square
History: New public space
Architectural feature: Combined square and building design

In the midst of this high, dry Sicilian plain, the urban spaces of Gibellina rise like a mirage in the swirling heat. Beautifully proportioned and empty, they stand like a stage waiting for a performance to start. The city space sequence is an attempt to create a collective urban identity in an area of almost suburban, uniform character.

Public spaces in Gibellina
1:5,000

Gibellina
1:50,000

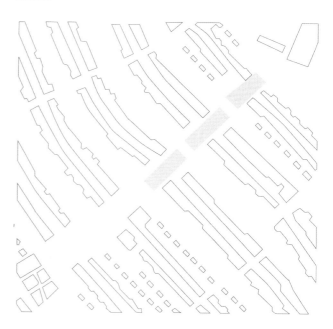

Newly built urban spaces, area: 5,300 m²
1:5,000

212

Course of space seen from Piazza Rivolta
del 26 Giugno 1937 towards Piazza Fasci
dei Lavoratori and Piazza Monti di Gibellina.

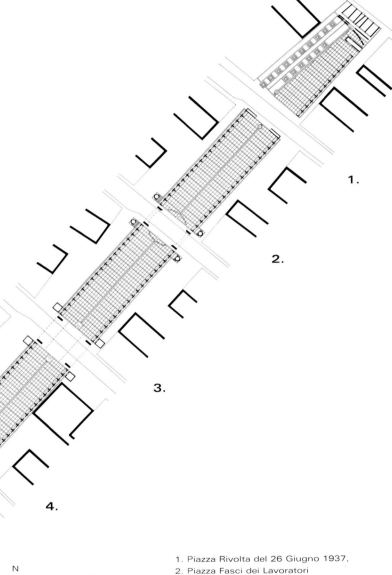

1.

2.

3.

4.

5.

N

10 20 30 40 50 metres

1:2,000

1. Piazza Rivolta del 26 Giugno 1937,
2. Piazza Fasci dei Lavoratori
3. Piazza Monti di Gibellina
4. Piazza Autonomia Siciliana (not built)
5. Piazza Portella della Ginestra (not built)

Gibellina is a small, completely new town tucked into the dry, hilly landscape of western Sicily. It was built on a bare field after an earthquake destroyed the original medieval town in 1968. The town was designed primarily with low-rise semi-detached buildings along winding streets. Architects Franco Purini and Laura Thermes designed five urban spaces to tie the residential streets in a diagonal axis, but only the first three have been built.

The space sequence is introduced by an "empty" building that forms the back wall for Piazza Rivolta del 26 Giugno 1937. The space opens out on the other side to palm trees planted systematically in small step pyramids. The sequence continues with Piazza Fasci dei Lavoratori and Piazza Monti di Gibellina, which are precise and beautifully proportioned city spaces created by erecting a row of screens that give them the feeling of a Greek agora. The screens are fitted with niches that provide shady seating. Through the portals in the screens, the residential streets continue diagonal to the course of space, which is divided into clearly defined squares. The plan was for the space sequences to continue with Piazza Autonomia Siciliana, and be concluded at the other end by Piazza Portella della Ginestra, where the town marketplace was to be located.

The walls of the spaces are heavily perforated with door openings, creating a semitransparent demarcation between outside and inside. Outside are the residential streets and an empty space between the screens and the adjacent buildings. Inside is the square itself, executed in fine materials: a floor of black basalt divided by light travertine and walls of brittle golden tufa.

The screens create a beautiful framework and strong spatial identity, but the site lacks urban activity along the edges of the square, which would give it the much needed gravity and sense of purpose. The site gives the strong impression of being an empty architectural stage, unfortunately one that has inspired neither actors nor audience to make their own.

Above: In the background, the "empty building" with what appears to be an ancient ruin in front of it. The ruin is actually a new interpretation of traditional Sicilian architecture and hides an electrical installation.

Right: The "back" of the space. The screen with many entrances seen from the outside.

Far right: The "empty building" from behind.

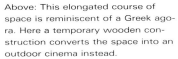

Above: This elongated course of space is reminiscent of a Greek agora. Here a temporary wooden construction converts the space into an outdoor cinema instead.

Above: A narrow passageway runs along the top storey of the screen.

Middle: All of the niches have benches of travertine marble.

Below: The floor of the square is black basalt with light travertine stripes.

Piazza Tartini

Piran, Slovenia. 1992
Architect: Boris Podrecca

Location: City centre
Type: Main city square
History: Renovated public space
Architectural feature: Surface treatment

The main square in Piran was originally a dock that was later aban-
doned and reworked into a square with a fine view of the harbour.
The main element in the renovation of the square is an elegant
white oval that unifies the irregular space and organises its fur-
nishings.

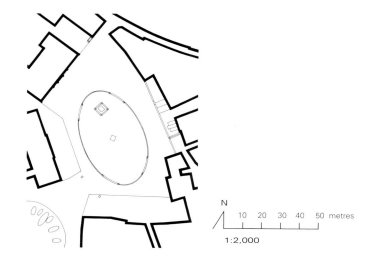

N   10   20   30   40   50 metres

1:2,000

Piran
1:50,000

Piazza Tartini
1:5,000

Main pedestrian zone: 1,500 m²
1:5,000

216

The irregular shape of the square is unified by the large white oval with a statue of Guiseppe Tartini. One side opens to provide a fine view of the harbour and the Adriatic sea.

Above: The white oval in the middle gives the square a clear identity.

Right: The light fixtures and benches are integrated into a unified design that provides a stationary activity zone along the edge of the oval.

Piran is attractively situated in the province of Istria on the Adriatic coast. The city has about 5,000 inhabitants and is an old port with buildings from many historical eras. The site of the present Piazza Tartini used to be a protected dock that opened towards the sea in the southwest corner. In time the harbour moved further out and the dock was abandoned, later acquiring its present function as the main square. The city space is irregular in shape and surrounded by buildings of very different character. In the northern corner is a Venetian building from the 1500s, on the east side St. Peter's Church from the 1300s and in the northwest corner a distinctive palace from the 1900s. On the square itself is a monument to the violinist Guiseppe Tartini, who was born in one of the buildings on the square, which was later named after him.

In the original drawings for the renovation of the space, the old dock was marked in the floor of the square, but that idea has not yet been carried out. The architect, Boris Podrecca, unified the irregular shape of the space by giving it a slightly arched oval in white travertine in the centre. A wind wheel is centred in the oval. The lighting fixtures and seating furniture are integrated into the edge of the oval, one of the stationary activity zones of the square. Another border zone was created along the edge of the surrounding buildings through sculpturally designed details in the form of a snail and several small fountains.

Above: The monument to violinist Guiseppe Tartini from 1879 in the background.

Below: Several sculptural details form the secondary edge along the facades to the east. The entrance to St. Peter's Church is visible in the background of the pictures left and right.

Cloud Gardens

Toronto, Ontario, Canada. 1993
Architects: Baird/Sampson Architects
Landscape architects: Milus, Bollenberghe, Topps, Watchorn
Artist: Margaret Priest

Location: City centre
Type: Recreational square/urban garden
History: New public space
Architectural feature: Composite character

Cloud Gardens is a new urban park with a dramatic story to tell in a limited space. The story relates the construction and demolition of the city landscape and nature's reconquest of the abandoned urban fragments. The park tells about the life cycle of an urban area and is a natural framework for the monument to the workers of the construction industry.

N

10 20 30 40 50 metres

1:2,000

Toronto, Ontario
1:200,000

Cloud Gardens
1:5,000

Area: 4,550 m²
1:5,000

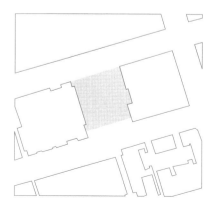

Cloud Gardens sustains a dialogue between its several distinctive elements. An ever-changing, partially demolished urban landscape is juxtaposed against an idealised natural landscape.

221

Cloud Gardens is the result of a public architecture competition. The park is a recreational element in a large urban development project comprising office buildings, shops, underground shopping centres and car parks that extend three urban blocks in downtown Toronto. The park was developed as an urban oasis in the midst of this large complex. Under the park are shopping galleries and underground parking. Ventilation shafts and access ramps have further complicated the design of the park.

The park project sprang from this rather special location and the dramatic and hasty urban conversions that take place in a large city.

The park has two main characters. Towards the east is a mixed urban landscape of buildings, ramps, stairs and stone surfaces. The urban elements build towards the surrounding taller buildings, communicating differences in height through terracing. A winter garden and a five-storey waterfall are prominent elements in this part of the park.

The west side of the park consists of a garden with benches, paths, grass surfaces and shady trees. Together the elements of the park express both the building of a large city and its decline, as depicted by ramps and terrace walls that seem to build towards the surroundings while deteriorating at the same time. The second element of the park, the green garden landscape, reflects nature's desire to reconquer abandoned structures in urban areas.

One element in the building program was the building of a monument to construction industry workers. The monument, designed by Margaret Priest, is on the east side of the park, a network of steel as the stylised symbol of craftsmanship and construction. The park won the Canadian Architecture Award of Excellence and The Governor General's Award for Architecture.

Above: The northeast corner of the park houses a fertile winter garden high above the rest of the park and the ramp to the underground car park.

Below: The winter garden casts a soft intriguing light into the darkness.

Above, right: Precise details mark the juxtaposition of landscape, stone floor, river and ramp in the southeast corner of the park.

Above and right: The winter garden, staircase and ramps facilitate a transition to neighbouring buildings. The steel framework with the monument to construction industry workers is also included in this transitional zone.

Village of Yorkville Park

Toronto, Ontario, Canada. 1994
Architects: Oleson Worland Architects
Landscape architects: Martha Swartz, Ken Smith &
David Meyer

Location: Historical neighbourhood close to city centre
Type: Recreational square/urban garden
History: New public space
Architectural feature: Composite character

Village of Yorkville Park is an oasis of green in the richly traditional Yorkville quarter north of Toronto's city centre. The composite character of the park is also a retelling of the history of the area and of the richly varied Canadian landscape. It is a combination botanical garden and interactive learning experience. The design with its many cross-sections is rooted in the residential structure of the old Yorkville village.

Toronto, Ontario
1:200,000

Village of Yorkville Park
1:5,000

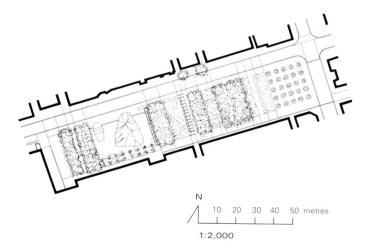

N
10 20 30 40 50 metres

1:2,000

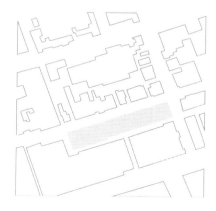

Area: 4,150 m²
1:5,000

Village of Yorkville Park from the east. The park is divided into many cross-sections that reflect the rhythm of the original semi-detached houses in the area. In the foreground is a grove of pines with "fog blowers" that envelop the trees in a cool misty shroud on hot summer days.

Full of character, Village of Yorkville is one of many such urban areas that make up the metropolis of Toronto. With its old traditional buildings and location just north of the city centre, Yorkville is a very attractive urban area. After the establishment of an underground train station in the middle of the area, the site above the station was used as a car park for many years. An international architecture competition in 1991 instigated the plans to establish an untraditional urban park on the site and by 1994 the old car park was history.

The park contains many design elements and layers of meaning due to the wide scope of the plans for it. Key design objectives were to reflect the Victorian scale and character of the area, to introduce national landscapes and flora, to offer a rich variation in spatial and sensory experience, and to provide good pedestrian connections. This extremely demanding program has been met by designing a long series of planted bands, pedestrian lanes and courses of space across the elongated, rectangular space. This division of the park into sections is based on the rhythm of semi-detached houses built in the area previously. Thus new city gardens recreate the size and character of the old market gardens of the townhouses. The Victorian tradition of planting gardens with trees and plants from surrounding landscape has also been continued, and this is one of the stories the park has to tell. Another bigger story is its reference to the majestic Canadian landscape stretching from coast to coast. The foggy landscape of pine tree forests in Nova Scotia in the east, Ontario's forests and lakes in the middle, and the prairie and Rocky Mountains to the west. All of these interpretations are found in the park, whose untraditional design reflects these different themes from swirling fog to an imported mountain cliff. The park contains 90 different types of plants and is well equipped with seating options in the form of benches and chairs that can be moved from landscape to landscape.

Left: View of the park from the west. The park is the transition between the tall buildings in the south and the low semi-detached houses in the north. A key theme in the design of the park is its division into highly varied landscapes, each reflecting a different Canadian landscape type. Small spaces within the larger sections provide popular recreational places.

Above: Horizontal steel structure with a flowing curtain of water that turns to icicle formations in winter.

Above: The park seen from the northwest. In the foreground, an entrance to the underground train, and behind that, the rocky cliff shipped to the park in 135 pieces and carefully reassembled.

Below: The eastern section of the park represents the fog-shrouded Canadian pine forests. Vertical poles spray tiny particles of water that provide refreshing coolness during the hot summer months. At night the "fog blowers" appear like illuminated posts in the forest landscape.

227

Place Berri

Montréal, Quebec, Canada. 1992
Architects/landscape architects: Peters Jacobs and
Philippe Poullaouec-Goniden
Artist: Melvin Charney

Location: District outside the historic city centre
Type: Recreational square
History: New public space
Architectural feature: Composite character

Place Berri is not an ordinary square, but an informal oasis in the middle of Montréal, where people relax during the summer in T-shirts and shorts, as if they were at the beach. The area is divided into a series of rectangular fields, each with its own character: A gravel space, a grassy landscape with streams in sculptural shapes running to a rocky beach, and a stone surface that is the actual square.

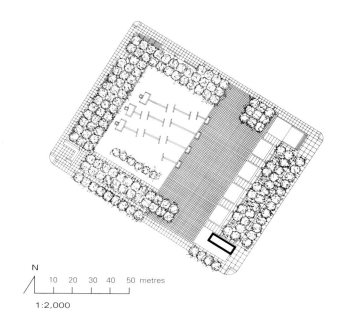

N

10 20 30 40 50 metres

1:2,000

Montréal
1:200,000

Place Berri
1:5,000

Area: 10,800m²
1:5,000

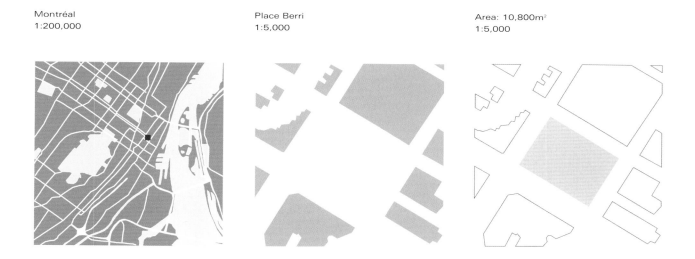

Place Berri northwest to southeast. The
square is divided into several fields, each
with a distinctive character. Far left is the
gravel floor, followed by a green landscape
containing three sculptures. To the right, the
stone floor and recreational area.

Montreal, one of the largest cities in Canada with three million inhabitants, is located in the Province of Quebec in eastern Canada. The city is named for Mont Royal, a distinctive range of volcanic hills that dominates the urban landscape and break its otherwise regular network of streets. The right-angled urban pattern is characterised by extensive blocks laid out with their long sides in a northwest direction towards the Saint Lawrence River.

In addition to its distinctive street system, Montreal also has 29 km of underground pedestrian passageways with shops and restaurants connected to the metro stations. Place Berri is a landscaped square located at Rue Berri west of the old part of Montreal. It is an area of mixed urban functions located close to Université du Québec and incorporating a metro station.

Place Berri is located in the Latin quarter, a lively part of Montreal, surrounded by offices, shops and a hotel. One corner has a sidewalk cafe and an entrance to Montreal's underground rapid transit system, which also connects to the large underground street network that stretches under the nearby buildings with shops and restaurants.

The square is edged by rows of trees screening it from the heavy traffic on the surrounding streets. A series of varied rectangular surfaces with different characters divides the square into fields. The uppermost field is composed of trees standing in a reddish gravel surface, followed by the grassy slope with its symbolic "rivers." Their sources are the three sculptures by Melvin Charney, which stand like scaffolding supporting pieces of building facades and street network "hung out to dry." Water courses through the cast gutters running here and there beneath the terrain through sculptural basalt blocks that serve as supports for stationary activity on the grass verge. The "rivers" flow towards the "beach," a large stone surface covered with warm, pink granite. The granite surface is sunken 90 cm below the surrounding street level and is divided into large square fields of about 80 x 80 cm. In winter the sunken field is used as an ice skating rink, while in summer it becomes a stage for concerts and other outdoor performances. Where the grassy landscape meets the gravel and stone surfaces, a low retaining wall of polished black granite at seat level marks the transition. The lowest field in the square, which faces a row of shops on Rue Sainte Catherine, is furnished with benches beneath shady trees.

Since its change from car park to pedestrian square, Place Berri has become a busy, popular meeting place, as well as one of the city's most used outdoor concert sites.

Above: The slightly sloping landscape is divided into "bridges" over "rivers," offering a variety of places to sit.

Far left: A supporting wall at seating height marks the transition between the gravel floor and the grassy landscape.

Left: The three sculptures in the background symbolise the development of the city's street network.

Above: The green landscape meets the hard stone floor at a stylised water's edge, a popular area for relaxing.

Above right: The stone floor has embedded points for attaching various installations.

Right: Here towards Rue Sainte-Catherine, benches under deciduous trees give the space more the character of a square.

Pioneer Courthouse Square

Portland, Oregon, USA. 1982-84
Architects: Willard K. Martin,
Martin/Soderstrom/Matteson

Location: City centre
Type: Main city square
History: New public space
Architectural feature: Surface and elements

*Pioneer Courthouse Square is a main square with design emphasis
on urban activity and meeting place functions. The square is a fine
example of a public space created on the initiative and energy of
the citizens of the town, who also raised a great deal of the fund-
ing through personal sponsorship. The names of the thousands of
donors are embedded in the red brick pavement that unifies the
square.*

Portland, Oregon
1:100,000

Pioneer Courthouse Square
1:5,000

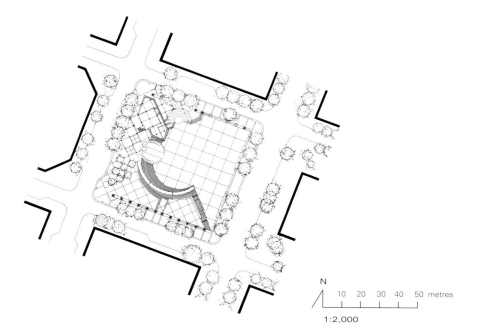

N
10 20 30 40 50 metres

1:2,000

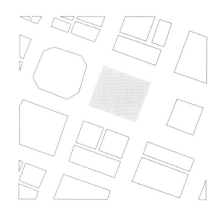

Central pedestrian zone: 5,100 m²
1:5,000

The large shell-shaped ramp and step element in the middle of the photo links the two levels of the square and creates one of the most popular areas for sitting. The square is edged on two sides by rows of columns supporting glass roofs that keep wind and rain from passengers waiting for the tram.

Portland has a typical North American grid structure. However, the city blocks are considerably shorter than in most other cities: 200 x 200 feet (61 x 61 metres), which gives the city a different rhythm than the majority of North American cities. Pioneer Courthouse Square is centrally located in front of the city's old courthouse, and fills an entire block of the street network.

Buildings surround Pioneer Courthouse Square on all four sides, in most cases with open facades and urban functions at ground-floor level. Around the square are a department store, some hotels, banks and several shops, but the plaza itself is an independent element on a platform surrounded by streets on all sides. Tall columns edge two sides of the square and create a zone with room for waiting tram passengers. The city's tram lines and bus lines cross at the square, which is an important hub for public transport. Portland offers free rides on buses and trams to passengers in the central city zone.

The transformation of the site into a public square was based on an international architectural competition, which was won by the local architects, Martin, Soderstrom and Matteson. Pioneer Courthouse Square fills an entire block in the city grid, which was cleared to form this public space. A multi-storey car park used to be on the site, but the citizens of Portland had long pressured the City Council to use the space in a different way. Throughout the planning process, active citizen groups expended an enormous amount of effort to involve the public and private companies in realising the project. One important element was to ensure broad backing for the city's new square through private sponsorship of the individual elements. The benches and trees were sponsored by various companies, while the almost 50,000 red bricks covering the floor were sponsored by individuals. Each donation entitled givers to have their names embedded on bricks laid on the square.

Pioneer Courthouse Square is a multifunctional space, whose design idea

provides many different options that appeal to various types of users. The square is the central meeting place for the people of Portland, in part as a central traffic hub for the many passengers using public transport. However, the plaza is also the city's expansive living room, where people can relax for a while, meet friends, watch the city go by or just enjoy life. The square invites many different stationary activities along its edges, in the form of columns to lean against, pedestals and steps.

The terrain falls from the western to the eastern corner of the site, a problem solved by dividing the square diagonally in two levels. A shell-

Above: Most of the furnishing elements are designed to serve as secondary seating.

Far left: One of the tall columns has "fallen".

Left: The base of the "fallen" column contains a chessboard that provides a popular pastime.

shaped ramp and step configuration links the two levels and creates one of the most popular areas for stationary activities. The upper level contains a cafe with pergola and outdoor serving. A bookstore specialising in travel books was dug under the upper level of the square. Across from the bookstore is an information board that shows the directions and distances of destinations near and far. There is access to the ticket office for public transport through the main fountain.

The square contains several sculptures with reference to the weather in Portland: a gentleman with an umbrella, and a "weather machine", a sculpture that carries out brief mechanical "weather shows" based on meteorological information about changes in the weather.

In many ways Pioneer Courthouse Square represents a special function-oriented North American type of square, with the space divided into a number of areas and zones that invite various types of activities. This contrasts with European squares that place emphasis on simplicity in the design of the space and fixed furniture, so that the space offers an open stage for varying activities, rather than a furnished stage for more specific activities.

Above and right: The staircase/ramp element provides a popular area for waiting and watching whatever is happening on the square.

Below: Each red brick has the name of a donor stamped into the surface.

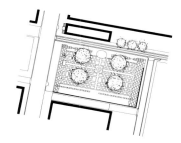

Welcome Park

Philadelphia, Pennsylvania, USA. 1982
Architects: Robert Venturi, John Rauch
and Denise Scott Brown
Landscape architect: G.E. Patton

Location: City centre
Type: Recreational/educational square
History: New public space
Architectural feature: Surface treatment

Welcome Park tells the story of William Penn and the founding of the city of Philadelphia. The stone-laid surface of the square depicts the plan of the city with its blocks and squares nestled between two rivers. Inscriptions and furnishing elements aid the narration. The square is built on the site of William Penn's former residence, Slate Roof House.

N

10 20 30 40 50 metres

1:2,000

Philadelphia, Pennsylvania
1:200,000

Welcome Park
1:5,000

Area: 1,250 m²
1:5,000

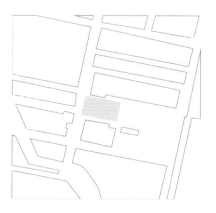

The theme for Welcome Park is the founding and early history of Philadelphia. The floor tells the story of the plan of the city, including its squares, represented by four trees.

Right: Section of the surrounding wall that relates the story of the city and William Penn.

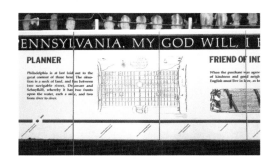

Next page: The inscriptions and decorative elements on the square are references to the history of Philadelphia and the life of William Penn. A bronze model on a granite pedestal marks the former site of William Penn's residence.

Below right: The plan of the city executed in dark stone with bands of white marble to indicate the street network. The monument to William Penn is centred in the square, while a bronze model represents the site of his former residence, Slate Roof House, to the left in the photo.

Below left: The plan of the city as theme is repeated in the architects' project for Western Plaza on Pennsylvania Avenue in Washington D.C. built in 1980-84.

Philadelphia plays a central role in the history of the USA, and many buildings and memorials connected to the liberation of the United States from colonial British power are preserved in the middle of the city. These monuments provide the framework for the Independence Historical National Park. Welcome Park is part of this national park, and in this connection welcomes and introduces visitors to the history of Philadelphia. The name of the park also refers to The Welcome, the ship that brought William Penn in 1682 to what later became the United States of America. The park was built in 1982 in connection with the 300th anniversary of his arrival, at the site where William Penn's home, Slate Roof House, used to stand.

Today the area is disjointed, dissipated by car parks, superfluous buildings and naked house gables. Into this untidy North American urban landscape, the park has been inserted as an independent, introverted urban project that has abandoned any hope of dialogue with its surroundings. The square is paved with dark stone blocks as the dominant element. The original city plan for Philadelphia is depicted in the floor by white marble bands representing the city streets, and the squares by beds around the four trees on the square.

Towards the east and west wavy lines that represent the Delaware and Shuyakill rivers conclude the street network in accordance with the original plan for the city. A monument to William Penn stands in the centre of the square, where the city's main streets Broad Street and High Street meet. A bronze model marks the former location of Slate Roof House. The square is delimited towards east and south by a wall about 1.80 m high, covered with enamel plates that describe how the city of Philadelphia came to be, as well as a broad outline of the life and work of William Penn. The wall serves as an educational blackboard with references to advertising and billboards in its design and placement in this modern urban landscape.

Three Squares in Qasr-Al-Hokm

Riyadh, Saudi Arabia. 1988-92
Project Coordinator: Riyadh Development Authority
**Design Team: Buro Happold, Ali M. Shoabi, Stefanno Bianca
and Rasem Badran**
Landscape architects: BBW & P

Location: Historic city centre
Type: Monumental square/urban square/marketplace
History: New public space
*Architectural feature: Sequence of spaces/combined square and
building design*

*The extensive renovation of the central Qasr-Al-Hokm district in
Riyadh provided the opportunity to build a sequence of new city
spaces in an area of symbolic importance. Two large squares are
connected by an elongated narrow link. The buildings in the area
were purpose-built and share a design language with traditional
roots. The new building frames the squares precisely, and furnishing is simple and streamlined, softened by water and palm trees.*

Three squares in Qasr-Al-Hokm
1:5,000

Riyadh
1:100,000

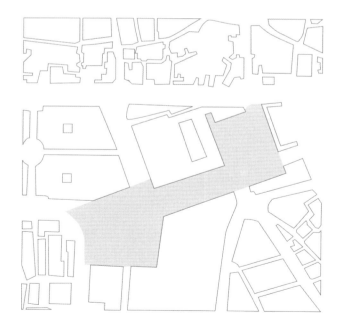

Three squares in Qasr-Al-Hokm, area: 33,000 m²
1:5,000

240

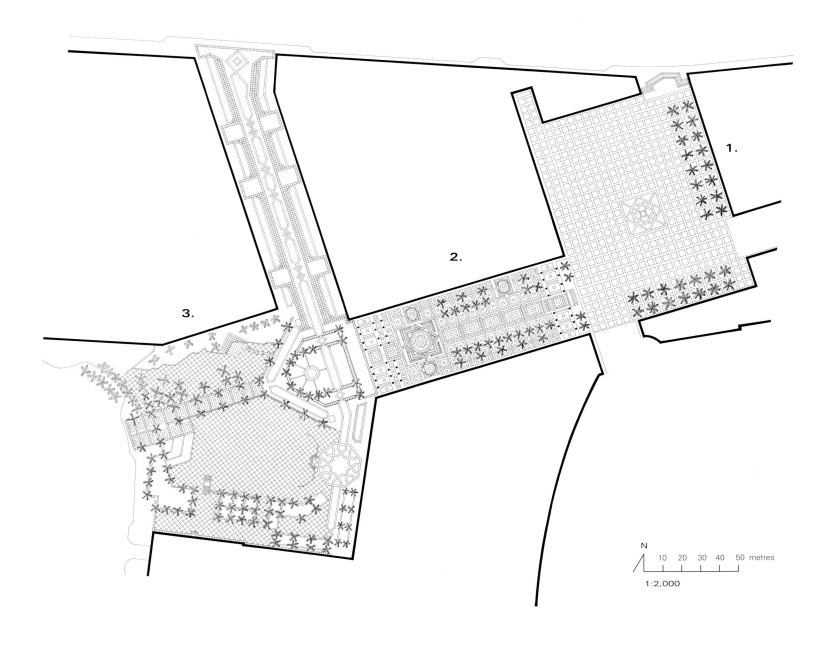

1. Maidan Al-Ada'al
2. Sahat As-Safat
3. Sahat Al-Imam Muhammad Bin Saud

N 10 20 30 40 50 metres

1:2,000

Maidan Al-Ada'al is the main square in Riyadh. Framed precisely by new monumental buildings, the walls of the square make a unified impression despite their very different functions. The square is furnished and planted with strict rows of date palms and benches. Many events are held here including market days.

Riyadh is the capital of Saudi Arabia and in a very short space of time has grown from a small traditional Arabian town into a metropolis with more than two million inhabitants. The city has been modernised and renovated in step with development.

Part of this conversion, started in 1983, was the extensive renovation of the historic centre of the city, the Qasr-Al-Hokm district.

The district is central in Riyadh, comprising approximately the area once protected by city walls. Qasr-Al-Hokm is the physical, historical and cultural centre not only of the city of Riyadh, but of all Saudi Arabia.

The district has been renovated in several phases, with the overall objective of clarifying the historical, cultural and religious position of the site, as well as expressing its symbolic significance for the development of Saudi Arabia as a modern state.

As the starting point for the design itself, the architects sought to achieve a high degree of integration between religious, cultural, commercial and administrative functions, as well as to develop a new but traditionally inspired design language with references to local architectural tradition. The first phase was carried out from 1983-88 and comprised the erection of administration buildings for the governor, police and city council. Several important monumental buildings were built during the second phase of the project from 1988-92, primarily the large Al-Imam Turki Bin Abdullah Mosque and the Palace of Justice, Qasr Al Hokm, which carries on an ancient tradition of representative functions at precisely this site. The second phase also included a large souq or market complex, a shopping street, and several reconstructions of historic landmarks, including parts of the city's original wall and two ancient city gates. A very important link in this phase was the establishment of a sequence of public spaces to connect the various functions in the area. Maidan Al Ada'al is the central square, not only for the area but also for the entire city. 14,000 m² of rectangular stone floor are framed by several of the new buildings.

Nozzles in the floor of the square provide an aquatic variety show during the day from tall columns to tiny jets and occasional intermissions.

The Al-Imam Turki bin Abdullah Mosque forms the west side of the square, while the Palace of Justice and the large souq serve as walls towards the south, east and north. Although the functions of these various buildings are obviously very different, they are executed in a common design language with uniform heights and the use of the same yellow brick as building material. The precision of the space is due to this coordination of architectural expression and building elements. The surface of the square is a large uniform stone floor of granite blocks in variations of grey laid in a quiet pattern. The green element is also very simple: double rows of date palms line the facades on the east and south sides of the square. Granite benches under the palms are the only furnishing.

The north side of the square has a large, decorative fountain. Hundreds of nozzles laid into the stone floor send jets of water four metres straight into the air, forming columns of cool, clear water. The fountain is programmed in a constantly changing pattern. Sometimes the only sign of water is the wet impression left on the surface or small jets of water a few centimetres high, which suddenly burst into columns of water taller than the people passing by. These aquatic columns activate the square on the days when it is not being used for ceremonies or other special events.

As the main square in Riyadh, during the year Qasr-Al-Hokm is the stage for many different types of events of both religious and secular character. The simple building architecture and large, open stone floor make the square a flexible framework for these many different activities.

Sahat As-Safat is west of the main square, and forms the connection between Maidan Al-Ada'al and the other large square in the area, Al-Imam Mohammed Bin Saud. The transition between Sahat As-Safat and the two large squares is articulated by a row of columns that carry a high pedestrian bridge connecting the mosque to the other buildings. This

Sahat As-Safat is an elongated space that connects the two main squares. Rows of date palms and streets lamps underscore its linear course.

Column arcades carrying pedestrian bridges cross Sahat As-Safat and mark the transition between the two large squares in the area.

Water is a recurring theme in the Qasr-Al-Hokm squares.

Above: A traditional fountain at the transition to Sahat As-Safat square.

Left: Jets of water at Maiden Al-Ada'al, courses of water and delta at Sahat Al-Imam Muhammad Bin Saud and drinking fountain at Sahat As-Safat.

combination of column arcades and closed bridges comprises the west and east walls of Sahat As-Safat and provides a distinctive transition between the three squares in the area. The character of Sahat As-Safat as a link between the two large squares is underscored by further defining the linear course of the space with rows of street lamps and date palms. Sahat Al-Imam Mohammed Bin Saud is the most westerly link in this sequence of new city spaces. Both in form and furnishing, this large square is more mixed in character and invites a more varied, more mundane type of daily activity. Like the other squares in the area, it has a granite stone floor in modified traditional patterns, but this time terraced and articulated by several water elements. One is an octagonal reflecting pool with a simple jet of water in the middle. A more fanciful course of water streams through part of the square into a delta in the stone surface and out into a recessed pool with nozzles and vertical jets of water. Although date palms are once again used as the green element, like the other elements on this square here they appear in a more varied pattern, some in rows, some in groups that refer symbolically to Riyadh as a shady palm grove, an oasis.

Al-Imam Mohammed Bin Saud square is the stage for many events during the year, here the important Eid Festival.

Near right: Reinterpretation of traditional designs and details, here at the entrance to Maiden Al-Ada'al.

Far right: Thumairi Street is one of the major shopping streets in the area, and also plays a role in the traditional Eid Festival.

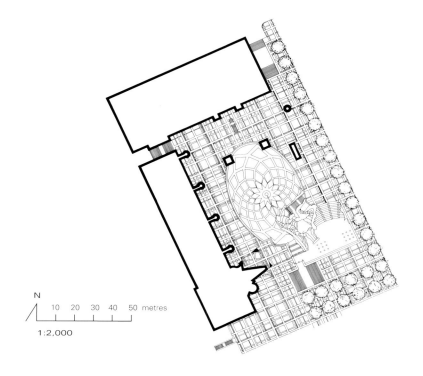

N

10 20 30 40 50 metres

1:2,000

Tsukuba Centre Square

Tsukuba, Japan. 1983
Architects: Arata Isozaki & Associates

Location: City centre in new town
Type: Main city square
History: New public space
Architectural feature: Combined square and building design

Tsukuba Centre Square is an integral part of Tsukuba Science City, a new urban development outside Tokyo. Together the city space and its buildings are a unified composition. The centre project contains a wealth of references to and commentary on urban ideals and urban architecture. For example, references to Piazza Campidoglio in Rome, but with notable design and colour contrasts. The square is a "non square" in a "non city" in poetic form.

Tsukuba, Japan
1:100,000

Tsukuba Centre Square
1:5,000

Pedestrian zone
1:5,000

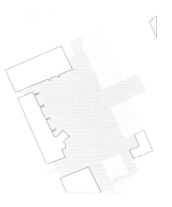

Above: Tsukuba's city centre seen from the north. The city was planned to reflect the ideals of modernism with free-standing buildings and a clear separation of roads and pedestrian paths.

Tsukuba Science City is a new urban development 60 kilometres northeast of Tokyo, with a university, science centre, service functions and housing. It was built from 1963-80 and is strongly influenced by the urban planning ideals of modernism, such as the allocation of areas by use, freestanding buildings, and the separation of roads and pedestrian paths. It is in the midst of this amorphous urban aggregation that Arata Isozaki, the winner of an architecture competition held in 1979, was entrusted with the design of a new urban centre. The centre's right-angle buildings house a hotel, concert hall, shops and restaurants, and form a wall for the city square towards the north and west.

The space is composed of three elements: a raised plateau of red ceramic stone in a regular square network of white tiles, a recessed oval area and a dramatic transition with steps, ramps and fountains between these two levels.

Just as the centre itself can be seen as a witty commentary on the surrounding "non city", in designing the square the architect worked with a wealth of references and contrasts. The recessed square has the form and dimensions of Michelangelo's Piazza Campidoglio in Rome, but whereas the Campidoglio is elevated, Tsukuba Square is recessed. Where the Campidoglio arches towards a central equestrian statue, Tsukuba Square is concave, centring on a depression, a drain for the water element of the square. Where Campidoglio has a dark surface with white stone bands, Tsukuba's colour composition is just the opposite.

The upper plateau and the oval square on the lower level in particular are quiet urban spaces, with very few visitors on ordinary days. The square does not invite urban recreation, and the great distances generally lessen the desire to walk in Tsukuba. In combination with the introverted functions of the centre and the many closed walls in the lower spaces, this means that Tsukuba centre neither wants nor can accept the role of a lively urban square. This too is a contrast.

Above: The design of the lower plateau of the square is an understated reference to Piazza Campidoglio in Rome. In contrast to the Italian model, Tsukuba Square has dark bands on a lighter surface and a fountain in the middle. Right: Piazza Campidoglio in Rome.

The transition between the two levels is handled by stairs, rocky landscapes and flowing water juxtaposed in organic forms that stand in contrast to the precise geometric surfaces and spaces of the square itself.

Swanston Street Walk

Melbourne, Victoria, Australia. 1992
Architects: Urban Design Branch, City of Melbourne

Location: City centre
Type: Promenade/pedestrian and public transport street
History: Renovated public space
Architectural feature: Street space emphasis/surface treatment

Swanston Street, Melbourne's main street, was converted into a pedestrian and tram street in 1992 as part of the city's efforts to prioritise pedestrians and limit private car traffic. The 900-metre-long, 30-metre-wide street space was treated as a traditional street profile with pavement, kerb and traffic lane in order to emphasise a boulevard character. The wide pavement nearest the traffic lane supports a length-wise furnishing zone with sculptures, decorative elements and urban furniture from the city's co-ordinated furnishing program.

Swanston Street Walk
1:20,000

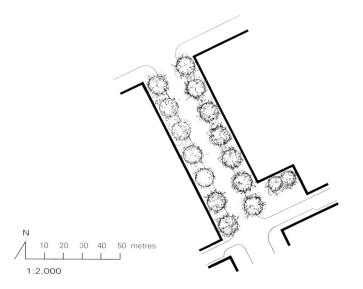

N
10 20 30 40 50 metres

1:2,000

Melbourne
1:200,000

Swanston Street Walk
1:20,000

Swanston Street Walk was closed to car traffic in 1992 and converted into a pedestrian and tram street. Trams and delivery vehicles share the 14-metre-wide asphalt traffic lane between the two 8.6 metres sidewalks.

Right: The 8.6 metre-wide sidewalk has a two-metre-wide furnishing zone adjacent to the kerb and traffic lane.

Lighting, benches and outdoor cafe service are here in this zone. Cafe tables and chairs are part of the city's furniture program, leased or purchased from the Town Hall.

Left: The city's furnishings include a wide variety of decorative elements. The top of a recessed column is the hallmark of the city library.

252

Swanston Street is Melbourne's historic main street, and formerly the major traffic artery for north–south traffic. As part of the city's general policy to prioritise pedestrians and limit private car traffic, the street was converted into a pedestrian and tram street in 1992, and the name was changed to Swanston Street Walk.

Swanston Street Walk comprises a 900-metre stretch through central Melbourne. The linear street is 30-metres wide and has two 8.6-metre-wide sidewalks on either side of asphalt traffic lanes with tram tracks running down the middle.

Architecturally efforts were made to emphasise the street space as a traditional city street. Other cities with broad pedestrian and tram streets, such as Karlsruhe, Germany, for example, laid pedestrian paving from facade to facade. In Melbourne, however, the decision was made to maintain a characteristic city street profile of pavement, kerb and traffic lanes. The advantage of this design is the clear symbolism and the strong visual emphasis of the linear course of space. In this particular case, the disadvantage is that the asphalt traffic lanes for trams and delivery traffic do not serve any other functions, and thus are considered rather too big and empty. After conversion Swanston Street Walk has been renovated completely with a new pavement in the local blue-grey bluestone, a type of basalt.

The city's furnishing program was also redesigned in the form of green steel benches, planters, screens, cafe tables and chairs. Lighting, trees and shrubbery have also been renewed and in time Swanston Street Walk will be a lush city boulevard with street trees.

A program for artistic decoration in the form of a linear "outdoor gallery" has been an important link in the transformation of the street. In this simple space with grey traffic lanes and blue-grey pavement, a number of surprising colours have been introduced including the fanciful decoration of lampposts and all types of housings for technical installations.

The establishment of Swanston Street Walk has been a considerable success for public transport as well as pedestrian traffic, illustrated by the fact that pedestrian traffic has increased by up to 65%. An extention of "the walk" toward the north will be completed in 2001.

The under-utilised traffic lanes in the middle of the street have been a temptation, and in 1999 the street was reopened to private car traffic from seven in the evening till seven in the morning. The new night traffic is limited, however, running to about 500 cars per night.

With Swanston Street Walk, Melbourne has gained a distinctive parade street and city boulevard, consistently executed on the basis of the intentions in the city's pedestrian-oriented public space policy.

Various types of street furniture in imaginative and colourful guises make a statement in the otherwise strict and simple grey and blue-grey surfaces of the streetscape.

Epilogue

A newcomer to the conference circuit is the walking conference. Conferences on car traffic and bicycling have attracted urban planners and politicians for a number of years, and now they are being invited to conferences on walking as well. The reason for this is well-founded concern about the future of walking options in cities. Walking has already been made impossible in some parts of the world. Public access is limited to car traffic and city life has disappeared. This trend is being discussed widely, and active policies to strengthen foot traffic are being formulated in many countries and cities all over the world.

It is not difficult to find supporting arguments. Walking is practical, environmentally friendly and cheap. It is also healthy and fun. Public transport systems presuppose that passengers are able to walk to and from stops, and even motorists become pedestrians when – and if – they ever get out of their cars. It is not difficult to find consensus for the idea that people will also need to be able to walk in cities in the future. This contention underlies the description of public strategies and public spaces in this book.

However, once we take the subject of creating good and worthy surroundings for foot traffic seriously, the next step is to ensure that people can sit down to rest and relax along the way. Benches and cafe chairs enter the picture. A selection of booths and shops also becomes relevant so that pedestrians can look and shop while they walk. The social aspect comes into play. Do people want to sit down to rest or drink coffee or watch the world go by? Often they want to do all three, and at the same time. They like to see and be seen by other people while they are out and about. City walking is a necessary key to urban quality, vitality and pleasure. The basis and the beginning for everything.

Vadare necesse est – walking is essential.

In the cities and public spaces described in this book, there are many different examples of how foot traffic and public life can be strengthened.

Examples range from simple pedestrian zones and oases to unified pedestrian and urban policies for an entire city. When efforts are limited to only a small part of a city centre, the results can be something along the lines of an overfilled amusement park, a theme park with the city as theme. The problem with this type of concentrated treatment is that it doesn't create enough good public spaces in the city and the ones it does create lack variety.

The integration of various functions is the key here. Good cities need a mixture of housing, shops, offices, institutions, schools and universities. Cities have to be in balance – and everything has to be accessible by foot.

Good balance is also desirable between types of traffic. In many older, dense urban streets, pedestrians and public life need all of the available space, while other streets can accomodate the coexistence of foot, bicycle and car traffic. Again, balance is the key. The boulevards of Paris and many pedestrian priority streets or streets with broad furnished sidewalks are good examples of coexistence.

The review of 9 cities and 39 public spaces also gives an impression of current trends in the architectural treatment of urban space, from simple almost classic public space projects to highly expressive, experimental projects. Function-orientation versus strong design-orientation can be seen as another set of contrasts.

The 39 public spaces presented in this book lie between these various extremes and present many combinations. And in many of the public spaces presented concern for pedestrians and urban recreational activities has been a high design priority.

Together the examples show that there is a rich and inspiring variety of solutions to the challenge of creating an urban framework as a meeting place for people.

The reconquering of the city as a people place is in process!

Index: 39 public space projects

Illustrations and photos

Acknowledgments

A great number of institutions, authorities and individuals helped make the collection of information and materials for this book possible. We would like to express our special thanks to the following people for their co-operation and willingness to help.

Foreword — Lord Richard Rogers of Riverside

Winning back public space — Peter Bosselmann, Otto Käszner, Eric Messerschmidt

9 cities – 9 public space strategies

Barcelona: — Olga Tarrasó
Lyon: — Jean-Pierre Charbonneau
Strasbourg: — Jean-Yves Bach, Valerie Attas, Sabine Chardonnet
Freiburg: — Reinhard Schelkes
Copenhagen: — Otto Käszner, Jens Rørbech, Jens Simonsen
Portland: — Peter Keyes
Curitiba: — Maria do Roco Quandt, Pablo Scalco, Simon Cerderholm
Cordoba: — Miguel Angel Roca, Roberto Ferraris, Pablo Bracamonte
Melbourne: — Rob Adams, Nathan Alexander, Brendan Devine

39 streets and squares

Gammeltorv/Nytorv, Copenhagen — Otto Käszner, Sanne Maj Andersen
Axeltorv, Copenhagen — Mogens Breyen
Sankt Hans Torv, Copenhagen — Sven-Ingvar Andersson
Ole Bulls Plass, Bergen — Arne Sälen, Karen Monnet
Gustav Adolfs Torg, Malmö — Sven-Ingvar Andersson
Main street in Kouvola, "Manski" — Mikko Heikillä
Broadgate Arena, London — Juan A. Alayo
Schouwburgplein, Rotterdam — Bo Grönlund
Konstantinplatz, Trier — Katja Beaujour, H. Monheim
Rathausplatz, St. Pölten — Rudolf Leitner, Boris Podrecca, D. Bartenbach
Champs-Élysées, Paris — Sabine Chardonnet
Place Vendôme, Paris — Pierre Prunet
Place Kléber, Strasbourg — Guy Clipot, Jean-Yves Bach, Sabine Chardonnet, Lisbet Bang, Marie Bonjour
Place de l'Homme de Fer, Strasbourg — Guy Clipot, Jean-Yves Bach
Place des Terreaux, Lyon — Jean-Pierre Charbonneau
Place de la Bourse, Lyon — Jean-Pierre Charbonneau
Plaça dels Països Catalans, Barcelona — Olga Tarrasó
Plaça del Sol, Barcelona — Olga Tarrasó
Parc del Clot, Barcelona — Olga Tarrasó
Plaça del General Moragues, Barcelona — Olga Tarrasó
Plaza de Carlos III el Noble, Olite — Zuhra Sasa, José Manuel Pozo, Mikel Murga
Piazza Matteotti, Catanzaro — Franco Zagari
Piazza Tartini, Piran — Boris Podrecca, Klaus Gerlach Jørgensen
Cloud Gardens, Toronto — George Baird
Village of Yorkville Park, Toronto — David Olson
Place Berri, Montréal — Georges Adamczyk
Pioneer Courthouse Square, Portland — Peter Keyes
Welcome Park, Philadelphia — Robert Venturi, Harris Steinberg
Three squares in Qasr-Al-Hokm, Riyadh — Abdulrahman al-Sari
Tsukuba Centre Square, Tsukuba — Tomiko Izumita
Swanston Street Walk, Melbourne — Rob Adams, Nathan Alexander, David Gordon, Hans Henrik Johansen

Project team

Project directors
Jan Gehl, dr.litt., senior lecturer in urban design
Lars Gemzøe, senior lecturer in urban design

Editor/research assistant
Zuhra Sasa, architect

Research assistants
Anne Marie Christensen, architect
Klaus Gerlach Jørgensen, architect
Ulla Rasmussen, architect
Louise Grassov, architecture student

Advisory group
The work of processing the collected material and planning the publication has been followed by a group of colleagues who kindly volunteered to review and discuss the project. The authors want to thank them profoundly for the ensuing discussions and valuable assistance concerning both contents and layout.

Peter Bosselmann, professor, University of California, Berkeley
Otto Käszner, former city architect of Copenhagen, Denmark
Eric Messerschmidt, architect, Danish Center for Architecture
Lisbeth Gasparski, senior lecturer in graphic design, School of Architecture, Royal Danish Academy of Fine Arts, Copenhagen, Denmark

We would also like to thank the many employees at the School of Architecture, Royal Danish Academy of Fine Arts in Copenhagen for their help and patience, and the many urban design students who spent their weekends and summer holidays to make this project possible.

English translation
Karen Steenhard

Layout
Stine Sandahl
Marie-Louise Teilmann
Consultant: Lisbeth Gasparski

Proofreading
Annie Foght
Lisbet Bang
Garry Wyatt
Joan Rose

Secretarial assistance
Karin Berg
Hanne Bendsen
Annie Foght

Other members of the team
Lene Rothe Andresen
Rune Christiansen
Sia Kirknæs
Karen Meelsen
Henriette Mortensen
Sun Muyan
Anne Line Møller
Eva Ravnborg
Britt Søndergaard
Matthew Toth

The research project "New Tendencies in Public Space
Architecture" was conducted from 1992-2000 at:

Centre for Public Space Research
Institute for Planning
School of Architecture
Royal Danish Academy of Fine Arts
Phillip de Langes Alle 10
DK-1435, Copenhagen K
Denmark
Phone: +45 32 68 60 00
E-mail: jan.gehl@karch.dk
         lars.gemzoe@karch.dk

The publication is available in a Danish version:
Nye Byrum
2.udgave, 1.oplag
The Danish Architectural Press
Copenhagen 2001
ISBN 87-7407-254-4

And in this English version:
New City Spaces
Third edition
Copenhagen 2003
ISBN 87-7407-293-5

Publisher:
The Danish Architectural Press
Overgaden oven Vandet 10, 1. sal
DK-1415 Copenhagen K
Denmark
E-mail: eksp@arkfo.dk
www.arkfo.dk